SECRETS OF THE SACRED
UNDERSTANDING THE BIBLE THROUGH INTELLIGENCE ANALYSIS

Rev. Dr. Keith Andrew Massey

Lingua Sacra Publishing

Secrets of the Sacred: Understanding the Bible
through Intelligence Analysis
Copyright © 2019 by Keith Andrew Massey

All rights reserved.
Published in the United States by
Lingua Sacra Publishing.
www.linguasacrapublishing.com
ISBN 978-1-7339934-0-1

Dedication

To Metropolitan John, who ordained me.

About the Author

Keith Massey, PhD, is the author of *Intermediate Arabic for Dummies,* a number of fiction novels, non-fiction books, and numerous academic articles on biblical, linguistic, and historical topics. For four years after 9/11, he worked as an Arabic linguist for the National Security Agency. He is currently an Eastern Orthodox priest and a language instructor.

Legal Disclaimer

The views and opinions expressed in this work are the author's and not that of the National Security Agency or the US Government.

Theological Disclaimer

The views and opinions expressed in this work are the author's, who does not claim to speak authoritatively for the Eastern Orthodox Church. The author is under the humble submission of his bishop in all theological matters.

Also By Keith Andrew Massey

Fiction

A Place of Brightness

Amor Vincit Omnia: An Andrew Valquist Adventure

Next Stop: Spanish

In Saecula Saeculorum

Non-Fiction

Intermediate Arabic for Dummies

Praying Our Fathers: The Secret Mercies of Ancestral Intercession

Top Secrets: Lessons for Success from the World of Espionage

Secrets of the Sacred: Understanding the Bible Through Intelligence Analysis

Introduction 1

Chapter One: HUMINT
(Human Intelligence) 21

Chapter Two: "Handing Over" Human
Intelligence 51

Chapter Three: SIGINT
(Signals Intelligence) 63

Chapter Four: Putting HUMINT and SIGINT
Together to Better Understand the Bible 81

Chapter Five: Image Intelligence (IMINT) 105

Chapter Six: Lost in Translation 111

Chapter Seven: Secret Codes (Decipherment) in
the Bible..145

Chapter Eight: Assessing the Eyewitnesses of
the Resurrection 163

Chapter Nine: Cracking the Code of the Number
666 179

Chapter Ten: King David: the Original Guitar
Hero...191

Chapter Eleven:
The So-Called "Horns" of Moses 195

Conclusion 201

Introduction

What does the Bible really say? What does the Bible really mean? Unlocking the secrets of the Sacred Scriptures has been the goal of believers for thousands of years. In this book, I will show you how the tools used by intelligence analysts can give us a refreshing new approach to studying the Bible.

In all humility, I may be uniquely equipped to present this paradigm of biblical study. I have a PhD in Biblical Hebrew and Semitic Studies, with a minor in Arabic. After 9/11, however, I worked for four years as an Arabic linguist at the Top Secret National Security Agency. After moving on from there to become a teacher, I was ordained and serve now as a priest in the Eastern Orthodox Church. I will describe my background in more detail just a bit later in this chapter.

I also firmly believe that study of the Bible through the lens of intelligence analysis can help

Protestant and Catholic and Orthodox Christians move closer, if not to a consensus, at least to a greater acceptance of one another's differences on several matters of theological controversy.

Spies in the Bible

Moses and the children of Israel had just escaped from Egypt. God now commanded them to enter into the land promised to their ancestor Abraham and possess it. Like any good military commander, Moses wanted some actionable intelligence on the nature of this land before they executed the order to invade. And so he sent twelve spies into the land, a leader from each of the tribes of Israel.

Goals of the Mission

Moses gave them a very specific list of intelligence requirements on which to return information. "Are the people there strong or weak, few or many," he asked. "What kind of land do they live in? Is it good or bad? What kind of towns do they live in? Are they unwalled or fortified? How is the soil? Is it fertile or poor? Are there trees on it or not? Do your best to bring back some of the fruit of the land."[1]

Results of the Mission

After forty days, the covert team returned from their mission with intelligence in the form of information and even physical samples of the area of conquest. They displayed to Moses and to the people a massive bunch of grapes that required two men to carry with the help of a pole! The team described the land as indeed flowing with milk and honey, but it was also occupied by powerful people with fortified cities. Some of the inhabitants were even described as having a giant stature.

One of the spies, Caleb, stated that, despite this information, "We should go up and take possession of the land, for we can certainly do it."[2] Another of the spies, Joshua, son of Nun, concurred (based on his support of Caleb in the following chapter).[3]

The other ten spies, however, insisted that the people of Israel could not conquer this land. And

---

[1] Numbers 13:17-20.

[2] Numbers 13:30.

[3] Numbers 14:7-9.

they spread a bad report through the people, such that the people disobeyed God's command to invade immediately.

How a Spy Reads this Passage

Theologians and biblical scholars will describe this primarily as a story of Israel's rebellion which then explains the people's subsequent forty year wandering in the desert. But as a former Arabic linguist with the Top Secret National Security Agency, I believe the story presents some interesting details perhaps only noticed when the story is considered in its espionage context.

The problem here was not the intelligence account itself. The entire team agreed that the land contained fortified cities and people of large stature. They also presented a common story on the fertility of the land. After all, they had returned agricultural products which attested to the abundance of the place.

The problem was not on the nature of the intelligence. This was a disagreement on how to interpret that report and what action, if any, could or should be taken as a result of that intelligence. Caleb and Joshua believed that nothing they had seen meant they could not immediately invade the land.

Interestingly, the success of this covert mission itself stands in stark contrast to the assertion that the Israelites could not invade. A team of twelve men had, after all, just spent forty days exploring the land and were able to return safely, even carrying a huge grape cluster on a pole. On the face of it, this fact alone should have made the people question just how perilous a place the Promised Land really was.

Intelligence Analysis and the Bible

As the above story demonstrates, the Bible certainly contains passages where the overall topic of intelligence analysis is not without a place in helping to explore the riches of a particular account. But I believe, since the Bible is a document composed in ancient languages, that it also lends itself to an examination using the tools of intelligence analysis. An NSA report about an intercepted phone call requires a different set of analytic tools than a CIA report about a covert source's claims. In the same way, the manner in which we read one of St. Paul's epistles should be different from ho w we read a narrative about St. Paul from the Book of Acts.

In this book I will describe the field of intelligence analysis and how it approaches various types of information derived from different espionage sources. Methods of biblical interpretation, developed over the course of the last two centuries or so, are not completely at odds with the techniques intelligence officers use to assess modern information.

I will show that the field of intelligence analysis can further our knowledge of the biblical text. This is because the field of intelligence analysis enjoys something that biblical scholarship never can—occasional confirmation (or refutation) of its findings. This enables intelligence analysis to refine its methodology to achieve ever greater accuracy for future interpretation.

How I Became a Biblical Scholar

I grew up on the blue-collar East Side of Madison, Wisconsin, the son of parents who themselves had moved to the "big city" from the agricultural town of Barneveld. In high school, I studied Latin for four years. I went to the University of Wisconsin in Madison and continued my Latin studies, graduating with a bachelor's degree in Classics (Latin and Ancient Greek).

I then completed a Master of Arts in Old Testament at Luther Seminary in St. Paul, Minnesota. I returned to Madison for another Masters in Biblical Hebrew and Semitic Studies, followed by a PhD in that field, with a minor in Arabic. Along the way, I published research in the areas of Biblical Hebrew language, Quranic studies, and interreligious dialogue.[4]

The Biblical Scholar Becomes a Spy

Then 9/11 happened. I felt duty-bound to offer my talents in the service of my country. And so I went to work at the Top Secret National Security Agency as a linguist. I am very proud to have

---

[4] 1993 "Dialogue of Creeds" in *ISLAMOCHRISTIANA* (Pontifical Institute of Arabic and Islamic Studies) by Keith Massey and Kevin Massey.

1995 "Semitic Quadriliteral Animal Terms: An Explanation," in *Journal of Northwest Semitic Languages* (University of Stellenbosch, South Africa) by Keith Massey and Kevin Massey.

1996 "Mystery Letters of the Quran," in *Arabica* (E.J. Brill Publishers) by Keith Massey.

1998 *The Concord of Collective Nouns and Verbs in Biblical Hebrew: A Controlled Study*. PhD Dissertation: University of Wisconsin: Madison.

served my country in this capacity during that time in history. I was awarded the Global War on Terrorism Civilian Service Medal for service performed in Iraq in 2004. I also received some training in the discipline of Cryptography while working there.[5]

As a scholar of biblical languages and studies, I began, even while working at the NSA, to notice important similarities and also differences between how we went about our jobs in the intelligence community and how people approach Scripture. Theoretically, both spies and biblical scholars should be concerned with exactly the same outcome—finding out the truth. My time working as a spy, having previously been a biblical scholar, led me more and more to the conclusion that applying espionage tactics to the study of Scripture could be a fruitful way to focus in on finding ultimate truth in the Bible.

The Spy becomes a Teacher

I had worked in a war zone for the NSA. I spent two years after Iraq working in the Counter

---

[5] For more details and anecdotes from my time at the NSA, read my book *Top Secrets: Lessons for Success from the World of Espionage.*

Terrorism Office there. And there came a point, after four years of such service, that I felt I had done my duty and that I was ready to move on to a quieter life. I resigned my position there to become a Latin teacher at a public high school. After I left the NSA, I published yet more academic articles on topics related to linguistics, as well as the book *Intermediate Arabic for Dummies*.[6]

Starting in 2009, I began to post my original research in the form of blog posts, to gain a wider readership than academic articles tend to get. A few of these articles, on matters specific to the Bible, are included later in this book. I have also

---

[6] 2002   "Letters and Mysterious Letters," contributor of article for *Encyclopedia of the Qur'an* (E.J. Brill Publishers).

2006   "A Second Look at Latin Secundus = 'Favorable'" in *Pomoerium* Online Journal, Vol. 5/2004-2006.

2007   "Vergilian Allusions In Newman's "Kindly Light," in *Newman Studies Journal*, Vol. 4, Issue 2, Fall 2007.

2008   "Further Evidence for an "Italic" Substratum in Romanian," in *Philologie im Netz* 43/2008, pp. 11-16.

2008   "A Latin Etymology for Romanian DA = Yes" in *Ianua. Revista Philologica Romanica*, Vol. 8.

2008   *Intermediate Arabic for Dummies*. Wiley Publishing.

published a number of fiction and non-fiction books.[7]

The Teacher Becomes a Priest

Following a decade of teaching and further research into biblical and theological studies, I was ordained a deacon and then a priest in the Eastern Orthodox Church. I continue to teach Latin while simultaneously serving as pastor of a parish.

I believe that my life experience uniquely equips me to explore the application of espionage methods to the study of Scripture. With academic

---

[7] **Fiction**

2009   *Next Stop: Spanish.*

2011   *A Place of Brightness.*

2012   *Amor Vincit Omnia: an Andrew Valquist Adventure.*

2012   *In Saecula Saeculorum.*

Non-Fiction

2014   *Praying Our Fathers: the Secret Mercies of Ancestral Intercession.*

2015   *Top Secrets: Lessons for Success from the World of Espionage.*

credentials in the area of biblical languages, a stint as a spy at the Top Secret National Security Agency, and the fact that I am an ordained clergyman, I will try to fuse together all these facets of my background to shed new light on certain aspects of the Bible.

Methods of Biblical Interpretation

For the past two hundred years or so, biblical scholars have been developing a number of interpretative methods in an effort to better understand the text of the Bible. In fact, these are basically the same tools that have been developed for study generally across all literatures. Now, I should here point out that some readers of the Bible reject these disciplines. If a reader ascribes to a view of biblical inspiration that assumes every word of the original text was fully inspired by God, they may view many of the modern methods as either unnecessary or even contrary to a proper understanding of Scripture. I believe that my approach can be fruitful regardless of what level of inspiration a reader believes in.

Textual Criticism

The most important field of biblical interpretation, in my opinion, is what is known as textual criticism. (The use of the word "criticism" here does not imply criticizing, rather it is the scientific term for studying the text from a certain perspective.) Textual criticism studies variations between different manuscripts and ancient translations in order to arrive at an understanding of what the most likely original text of the Bible really was.

An example of the need for textual criticism can be found in Genesis 4:8. The Masoretic Text (hereafter MT) of the Hebrew Bible (the version codified by Rabbinic Judaism) reads as follows in that verse:

> And Cain said to Abel his brother and it happened when they were in the field...

But the Samaritan Pentateuch (hereafter SP), a version of the Five Books of Moses preserved by the Samaritans, has something extra:

> And Cain said to Abel his brother, **'Let us go to the field'**. And it happened when they were in the field...

Interestingly, the Septuagint (a Greek translation of the Hebrew Bible somewhat older than the codification of the MT [hereafter LXX[8]]) is apparently reading from the same original Hebrew text found in the SP:

> And Cain said to Abel his brother, **'Let us go to the field'.**

What very likely happened is that at some point in the copying process, someone accidentally had their eye skip from one instance of the word "and" (Hebrew *waw*) and continued copying from the next one, thereby omitting an entire phrase in the manuscript that eventually was ratified as the MT.

The Bible translation you use very likely contains the extra phrase, even if the translators otherwise were working from the MT. But it should be acknowledged that reading the whole Bible as it was originally written requires, as it were, rescuing it from multiple manuscript traditions.

---

[8] LXX is the Roman numeral for 70, which is what the Latin word Septuagint means. This follows a tradition that 72 translators were involved in that translation project.

Source Criticism

If someone asks you how many of each animal went on Noah's Ark, the obvious answer is that they entered two by two! And that's exactly what the Book of Genesis says.[9] But if you read on, something rather confusing happens. We later read that the LORD[10] tells Noah to take *seven* pairs of all clean animals, and only a pair of those animals that are unclean.[11] Okay, so maybe the LORD has updated his instructions. But then, if you keep reading, we read once again that Noah brought only two of each, both clean and unclean, just as God had earlier commanded him.[12]

What in the world is going on here? If you pay close attention to the details, you will notice when I reported seven pairs of animals, I described that order coming from "the LORD." It turns out that the Noah story is actually a blend of two different accounts of the story, one of which always calls

---

[9] Genesis 6:19.

[10] Putting the word LORD in all caps like that is a convention for representing the divine name, which in Hebrew is spelled with the consonants YHWH.

[11] Genesis 7:2.

[12] Genesis 7:8-9.

God "the LORD."[13] The other account only calls him "God."[14] And the reason the source that called God LORD makes sure there are seven pairs of clean animals on board, is that after they finally get back on dry land, Noah makes a sacrifice of every clean animal.[15] If there were only two of each animal, and then Noah slaughtered one of them, those species would have gone extinct!

Other Methods of Biblical Criticism

There are a number of other sub-divisions of biblical criticism, such as form criticism,[16] rhetorical criticism,[17] and redaction criticism,[18] to

---

[13] Scholars call this the "J Source," after the German Jahwist, derived from the name YHWH.

[14] This part of the Noah story comes from what is called the "P Source," after "Priestly." The P Source believed that the Divine Name was given only much later to Moses, and therefore was not used in any pre-Mosaic account.

[15] Genesis 8:20.

[16] Form Criticism focuses on understanding that the current text is an assemblage of a variety of forms, such as myths, hymns, and legends, which come to us from an oral transmission, which fact could shed light on their original meaning.

[17] Rhetorical Criticism focuses on how various forms of speech are employed with an interest in not just informing an audience but entertaining and ultimately persuading.

name just a few.[19] These and many other methods of biblical interpretation ultimately aim to do the same thing as intelligence analysis—to better understand the text and, ultimately, the truth. But the reason this wide array of methods is applied to the Bible is that the Bible is no simple document.

No matter what one believes in terms of inspiration, there is no denying that the Bible is not just one book. It is dozens of different books that also come from widely different times, places, and languages.[20] And so, just as you wouldn't read a cookie recipe the same way you would read a love poem, you know instinctively that one of the Psalms conveys meaning differently than one of St. Paul's letters. All of the methods described above have been developed in an attempt either to understand the biblical texts in their original

---

[18] Redaction criticism focuses on the role of the typical biblical author as, in fact, being that of an editor to a great extent, compiling earlier sources, albeit with their own desired emphasis.

[19] For an excellent source covering all facets of biblical criticism, see *Biblical Exegesis*, by John H. Hayes and Carl R. Holladay (2007, Westminster John Knox Press).

[20] The Bible was written in Ancient Hebrew, Aramaic, and Koine Greek, with scattered words in other languages such as Philistine and Latin; its composition spans at least a thousand years.

intent or to foster their use in a modern context within a faith community.

Intelligence Analysis

As I said above, in many ways intelligence analysis and the various methods of biblical criticism are already at least trying to do the same thing. When an NSA linguist has to guess at a word where the message is corrupted, they are engaging in textual criticism. When a CIA analyst is trying to determine if a source's use of a particular word was significant, they may be engaging in rhetorical criticism.

I am going to show you how approaching the Bible through a combination of the disciplines of intelligence analysis can lead us to connections and insights that traditional methods of biblical criticism alone cannot. In particular, I will explore how teachings suggested to us by human intelligence sources both within and outside the Bible can lead us to a deeper knowledge of the truth when we confirm those teachings in the Bible.

In the chapters that follow, I will go into depth and detail on the various disciplines of espionage and talk about what each could bring to the study of the Bible. To give you a preview of what this will involve, I offer the following thoughts.

Human intelligence (human spies trying to get humans to share secrets) is focused on assessing the reliability and credibility of the information they obtain. Biblical scholars do not generally concern themselves with these criteria because more conservative scholars accept the entire Bible as true because it is inspired. More liberal scholars do not need the biblical accounts to be factually true in order to draw spiritual lessons. I will step outside the spectrum of "conservative" and "liberal" to instead argue that applying the same criteria spies do to their information lets us look at key doctrines and historical accounts in a whole new light.

Signals intelligence (secrets derived from intercepted communications) is concerned with determining what a piece of language actually means, so that any potential intelligence value can then be extracted and supplied to policy makers. It is certainly true that modern biblical scholarship seeks to use the latest linguistic research to properly understand the meaning of the biblical text. But I will explore, through signals intelligence, the concept that a strict focus on the ultimate meaning and original intent of the author/speaker is sometimes lost in modern biblical scholarship in an attempt to make Scripture "relevant" for today. I will argue that an application to the Bible of the precise methods I learned at the NSA regarding the translation, interpretation, and then reporting of intercepted communications can be a fruitful way to make this collection of ancient texts truly come alive for the modern world.

In this book I will also explore several other ways the world of espionage can help us better understand the Bible. These will include an in-depth look at what actually goes into the process of translation, since most people are not really reading the Bible at all, but rather someone else's translation (and, frequently, the translator's personal interpretation).

I will delve into the very exciting field of image intelligence (think spy satellites and high resolution images of enemy missiles), which potentially can make the Bible more vivid today than it has been since the time of contemporary readers 2000 or more years ago.

Finally, I will share an assortment of studies I have made into various aspects of Sacred

Scripture, applying everything I have learned through biblical languages as well as my time as a spy, uncovering what I believe are exciting truths which have been dormant for many centuries.

And so, if you are willing to accept this mission, turn the page to begin your orientation into the world of espionage and the Bible. Your first briefing is on human intelligence.

Chapter One: Human Intelligence (HUMINT)

Definition of HUMINT

Human intelligence is intelligence gathered by people interacting with other people. Now, such an interaction is not always a mutual sharing. For instance, if a spy somewhere manages to be sitting at a restaurant in the booth next to an intelligence target, and she overhears the target say something important, that is intelligence gathered by a person from a person. It's human intelligence. But, generally speaking, HUMINT usually involves someone sharing information directly with another person. And the person sharing the secret is generally doing so with a motive. Frequently the motive is money.

The New Testament contains a classic example

of someone passing on information of intelligence value in exchange for money. Judas led the temple authorities to the place where they could arrest Jesus in exchange for thirty pieces of silver.[21]

Who Conducts HUMINT?

Most HUMINT in the United States' intelligence community is conducted by the CIA. The fact that they have clandestine agents all over the world is hardly a secret, since you can apply to be a clandestine agent right on their website![22] And the job of such clandestine agents is to obtain information of intelligence value from other people. Theoretically it does not matter who the people are from which they glean their information. The only thing that matters is whether it has intelligence value. In other words, a diplomat from country A stationed in country B obviously knows things policy makers in the United States would like to learn. But if that diplomat talks too openly about state secrets when

---

[21] Matthew 26:14-16; 26:47-48.

[22] The CIA conducts HUMINT with its "Directorate of Operations (Formerly known as the Clandestine Service)." https://www.cia.gov/careers/opportunities/clandestine/index.html

he's had a few too many to drink, his butler might be the source of valuable intelligence as well!

While human intelligence is conducted primarily and formally by the CIA, there are other government agencies that do human intelligence in an unofficial capacity all the time. If a US diplomat, an employee of the State Department, is at a dinner in the country of his or her posting, and they learn something that may be of intelligence value, they are obligated to report such information.

What are the most important issues in HUMINT?

Usually, HUMINT is information one person wants another person to have. The problem is, there are multiple motivations one could have for sharing information. One of them may indeed be a desire to mislead! In fact, there have been cases in the history of espionage in which a spy has told another spy true information merely to establish credibility for a long term plan to do substantial damage at a later date with misinformation.[23]

---

[23] A notorious example of this is the so-called "Double Cross System" run by British intelligence during WWII. Captured German agents who agreed to collaborate were fed legitimate

The point is, whenever a spy learns information from an asset, all we really know is that the asset wants the spy to have that info. We technically know nothing about the credibility of the information itself.

We all go through our day under what is known as the "truth bias." In other words, virtually everything people say to you all day long is true. And, for that reason, we receive information and incorporate it into our daily plans assuming it is true unless we learn otherwise.

I mean, imagine if you tried to function under the complete opposite of the truth bias. If everything you heard from everyone in your life was assumed to be a lie unless you learned otherwise, you would lose your mind in the exhaustion of chasing down confirmation of the information around you.

The problem for HUMINT is that we sometimes take in this information without subjecting it to appropriate scrutiny. In the category of HUMINT, we should be much more

---

information to report back so that eventual misinformation would be more readily believed. This plan is credited with the success of the D-Day Landing. See *Double Cross: The True Story of the D-Day Spies*, by Ben Macintyre (2013: Broadway Books).

discriminating about the potential for misinformation than in our day-to-day lives. And yet, in the history of espionage, credence has sometimes been given to information despite obvious red flags.

Perhaps the most famous recent example of an intelligence failure connected to the "truth bias" is the misplaced credence that was given to the intelligence source known as "Curveball." This man, Rafid Ahmed Alwan, had made claims to German intelligence regarding the Chemical Weapons capabilities of the Saddam Hussein regime in order to gain asylum and permanent residency there.[24] Information he supplied eventually was reported by Secretary of State Colin Powell to the UN in the lead up to the Iraq War. And his claims were ultimately found to be fabricated.

Don't Believe Everything You Read

CIA reports contain an automatic caveat at the end, to the effect that whatever information this report contains may have been provided with the

---

[24] "Iraq war source's name revealed." *BBC News*, November 2, 2007.
http://news.bbc.co.uk/2/hi/middle_east/7075501.stm

intention to "deceive or mislead." Hopefully the presence of this caveat leads policy makers to take the information provided for exactly what it might be worth—which could be, in some cases, a grain of salt.

One final anecdotal comment. As of the time I left the NSA, some CIA reports that I saw WERE BEING RELEASED IN ALL CAPS! Now, maybe they were only in all caps in the systems I had access to. Maybe, like NSA reports, they were actually released to policy makers in a nice professional office style.

But if all readers of these reports were seeing them in all caps like I was, that is a potential problem. Anything written in all caps seems to scream at you. I hope that the effect of all caps did not result in a bias wherein the font itself seemed to imply urgency.

Circular Reporting

Another issue analysts have to remember when weighing the veracity of HUMINT, and in fact this applies to other disciplines within the intelligence community as well, is the possibility of what is known as circular reporting. This is also known as False Confirmation. Multiple sources all stating the same information are not necessarily independent voices.

For instance, if you told all your friends a story, and they all went and told the story to their spouses, the fact that the story was related by a number of different people does not make it more reliable. It came from a single source.

Circular Reporting is precisely what makes false rumors seem credible. Once the rumor really takes off, you are hearing it from multiple, seemingly unconnected, sources. You think to yourself, that's the third person I've heard that news from today, so it must be true. But that false rumor could have started with one source, who intentionally fed misinformation to someone, knowing it would take off like wildfire.

The concept of Circular Reporting will also be important when we study how manuscript copyist errors are repeated generation after generation. Even if many traditions agree on a certain reading of the biblical text, it does not mean that that is what was originally written.

As well, an account about Jesus found in Matthew, Mark, and Luke is not therefore corroborated by three sources, since we know from biblical analysis that Matthew and Luke were both using Mark as their source text.

HUMINT: A Case Study

Let's use a hypothetical case to further explore what is involved in HUMINT. Sharon White is a CIA Clandestine Officer. She is stationed in Slobovia, under cover pretending to be a tourist visiting the famous ancient Roman ruins there. She approaches a man she recognizes from briefings. Colonel Black is known to love visiting these sites. He is also known to be in on planning the possible invasion of one of Slobovia's neighbors. Now, the United States obviously wants to know when that invasion is supposed to happen. Even if we plan on remaining neutral, we at least want to warn our embassy staff in both countries.

She approaches Colonel Black and slips an envelope into his hand. He looks at her curiously as she quickly walks away. He opens the envelope at home and finds ten hundred dollar bills and a note: "Another hundred thousand for the date of the invasion. Meet me back at the ruins tomorrow at noon."

Now, here's where maybe you're wondering why we would assume that this Colonel Black really would betray his government just for a little money. In practice, Agent White would probably not be making this contact without some other ace up her sleeve. She may know from her briefings that Colonel Black is deep in debt from a gambling problem. She may know that agents of another country are blackmailing him to keep a marital affair secret. Even so, what she is doing is by no means safe. She could easily go to the ruins tomorrow and find herself arrested for an attempted bribe and espionage.

But, this contact goes as planned. They meet the following day at noon. She hands him a thick envelope containing a hundred thousand dollars. He hands her an envelope with the following note: "02/03/2019."

Alright. We now have information acquired through HUMINT about the upcoming invasion. The analysis can begin. You may think this is a no-brainer. We have a date. February 3rd, 2019. But right there we may have a problem. Slobovia, like most European countries, tends to write the day first and then the month. So this might be March 2nd, 2019. Or did Colonel Black, knowing that Agent White is an American use the system he knows she uses? But even if we cannot solve this initial problem, the information is still quite valuable. We may very well see February 3rd come and go and then be able to confidently assert that the attack will happen on March 2nd.

Or can we? You see, we often make the mistake of taking all information at face value. Here is where our own human psychology becomes a factor in intelligence analysis. As I noted above, we all go through our day receiving information from others and reacting accordingly. And, with actually few exceptions, that information is true. Sure, from time to time we catch someone in either an inaccuracy or even an outright lie. But the random lies we encounter do not overturn our tendency to believe information. So, in the case of Colonel Black's message, all we really know about this information is that this is what he gave in exchange for a hundred thousand dollars. Perhaps he assumes that Agent White intends to pass this information to Slobovia's enemies. Maybe the actual invasion is on January 4th and now they think they will have the element of surprise. There is also always the possibility that Colonel Black legitimately believes that this is the date of the invasion and someone higher up than he knows otherwise.

Making Sense of HUMINT

So, what is the value of any human intelligence if every bit of it could be wrong? Well, in practice, it's not always wrong. It's frequently true. If Colonel Black really does have a gambling problem, he's going to need money again someday. And if he gives our agent inaccurate information, he's going to know that she won't trust him next time. This is precisely why human sources are only considered trustworthy after they have supplied information that is later corroborated.

And the fact that a human intelligence source may not be accurate leads the CIA to put important and clear qualifications on their reports. After the report states the information the source provided, the report may state that "Source has in the past provided information that was corroborated." But then the report, as I mentioned above, will always state that "this information may have been provided with the intent to deceive or mislead."

Human intelligence and the Bible

No matter what you may believe about the ultimate inspiration and authority of the Bible, on the face of it, Scripture is information provided by a person intended for a person. As such, viewing certain parts of biblical material through the lens of HUMINT can provide us with an interpretative paradigm to assess the information.

When reading the Bible we can and should ask some general questions regarding the meaning of the information.

1) What does the text actually say?

In order to interpret Colonel Black's message, we were forced to initially translate the numbers into a date. And right off the bat we faced an ambiguity. Now, Colonel Black did not probably intend to convey an ambiguous message. But he sure did anyway. In the same way, an author writing in ancient Hebrew in the year 587 BC intends to convey information to his reader. But you and I, thousands of years later and not being native speakers of ancient Hebrew, were not his or her intended reader.

The take away is that we have to accept that the distance in time and culture could easily create situations where information intended by the author, particularly by way of a nuance known only to native speakers, is not detectable by us today. In other words, the author could have been as clear as he or she could be, but it is still not clear to us, for precisely the same reason that we weren't sure about the date of the attack.

We are forced to accept that the Bible, as an authentic historical and linguistic artifact, is not something we can ever completely understand. We can understand it and appreciate it and be instructed by it in important ways. But it can never be our all sufficient source of knowledge.

2) Why is this information being shared?

Now, in the case of Colonel Black, we believe it is being shared because he needs our money. And to the extent that we can accurately assess that motive, we may be able to then apply varying levels of credence to the information.

In the case of the biblical text, there could be different levels of information sharing. And it is helpful to consider each and every filter through which that information passed before deciding what that information means.

Let's take as an example the story of Adam and Eve. Where did you get the information? Now, before you say Genesis Chapters 2 and 3, I'll point out that there is a more immediate filter through which you probably got it. You are likely looking at that story in an English translation produced in modern times. In the chapter "Lost in Translation"

I will discuss in depth issues related to the interpretation of intelligence that passed through translation on its way to the reporter. As for the people who translated that story from Hebrew for you, where did they get it? Well, they got it from manuscripts that people had laboriously copied by hand for centuries. Another consideration worth noting is that the whole reason it was copied and then translated for you is that a faith community believed it was something worth transmitting. We do eventually, possibly through the additional filter of someone who compiled the stories found in the Torah, arrive at our author. Our author also told that story for a reason.

Modern biblical interpretative methods approach the story of Adam and Eve from a number of different angles. Source Criticism would try to explain the story within the wider framework of the Jahwist materials. Form Criticism would perhaps compare the story to other etiologies.[25] And what does the field of human intelligence gathering tell us is the likely reason that our

---

[25] An etiology is a story that serves to explain why something is the way it is. An example of this is the playful claim that the Finger Lakes in New York were created by Paul Bunyan tripping and his fingers carving them out. It should be noted that in many cases etiologies are not actually believed in by the people that create them and pass them on.

author shared the story of Adam and Eve?

After assessing all the possible motives our author may have had for putting this story down and then transmitting it, HUMINT analysis would come to what, in the modern world, may seem a controversial conclusion.

That author told the story of Adam and Eve for the primary reason that—they believed it was true.

They lack any of the traditional motivations by which a human source would seek to mislead. And so we have to take the author at face value. Now, mind you, I am not saying here that you have to believe that the story of Adam and Eve actually happened exactly as Genesis 2 and 3 record.[26] But I am saying that casting a modern interpretation on it simply because our views of science are not in agreement with theirs is not fair to our ultimate human source for that information.

So rather than spiritualize the accounts, I would prefer to receive the information as exactly what it is. Genesis 2 and 3 record for us what a human source several centuries ago in the Hebraic

---

[26] I do not personally subscribe to a literal and historical interpretation of all Scripture. I profess belief that most things in the New Testament happened as recorded (meaning I accept the New Testament at face value, but do not feel the need to harmonize minor inconsistencies between parallel accounts).

tradition believed was the story of human creation.

In other words, I am saying that there is a difference between reading the biblical account and reading an allegory *into* the biblical account. We can read anything—the Bible, Hamlet, or last night's lottery numbers—in an allegorical fashion. But that does not make them allegories. When we allegorize the biblical account of creation, we are engaging in an interpretive exercise prompted by a world view from outside the biblical text. Again, I am not saying that if you believe in God that you have to believe in a literal interpretation of Genesis. I do not personally ascribe to a literal interpretation of that text. But I am forced to conclude, based on the author's absence of any motive to be misleading, that the author believed in it.

That is not to say that there cannot be a use of Scripture that is spiritual instead of purely factual. I can simultaneously believe that the authors of Genesis actually believed in their creation narrative and also use it to draw a spiritual message that does not ascribe to its literal message.

Using Intelligence Analysis to Assess the Reliability of a Source

Perhaps the most important application of human intelligence methodology to the Bible will be to ultimately put Scripture itself to a reliability test. In order to assess how credible a source of intelligence is, and have a consistent way to describe that reliability, NATO countries use what is termed the Admiralty Code. First, the source is assigned a letter based on their reliability as a source:[27]

> **A - Completely reliable**: No doubt of authenticity, trustworthiness, or competency; has a history of complete reliability.
> **B - Usually reliable**: Minor doubt about authenticity, trustworthiness, or competency; has a history of valid information most of the time.
> **C - Fairly reliable**: Doubt of authenticity, trustworthiness, or competency but has provided valid information in the past.
> **D - Not usually reliable**: Significant doubt about authenticity, trustworthiness, or competency but has provided valid information in the past.
> **E - Unreliable**: Lacking in authenticity,

---

[27] US Army Field Manual 2-22.3, p. B1.
https://fas.org/irp/doddir/army/fm2-22-3.pdf

trustworthiness, and competency; history of invalid information.

F - Reliability cannot be judged: No basis exists for evaluating the reliability of the source.

Notice here, the letters should not be considered "letter grades" for how good a source is. This is strictly a ruling on how *reliable* a source is based on past performance. Arguably, a source termed "E" is to be trusted less than one with an "F," since the E source has previously demonstrated *unreliability*. The F source is presumably brand new and we do not yet have any basis for assessing their reliability. Even though it has an "F," it might be entirely true. We just do not have any reason to trust it yet.

Next the actual information presented by the source is itself assessed for its accuracy, based on factors such as its confirmation by other sources, reasonableness, and consistency with other intelligence:[28]

---

[28] US Army Field Manual 2-22.3, p. 2.
https://fas.org/irp/doddir/army/fm2-22-3.pdf

1 - Confirmed by other sources: Confirmed by other independent sources; logical in itself; Consistent with other information on the subject.
2 - Probably True: Not confirmed; logical in itself; consistent with other information on the subject.
3 - Possibly True: Not confirmed; reasonably logical in itself; agrees with some other information on the subject.
4 - Doubtful: Not confirmed; possible but not logical; no other information on the subject.
5 - Improbable: Not confirmed; not logical in itself; contradicted by other information on the subject.
6 - Truth cannot be judged: No basis exists for evaluating the validity of the information.

Similarly with the reliability letters, note that number 6 here is simply a score assigned with no way to yet evaluate the information, whereas with 5 we presumably have other information which implies the data we are currently studying is probably not correct.

Using this framework to study the reliability of Scripture, or any ancient text for that matter, presents interesting challenges not met when applying it to a modern day source a HUMINT agent may be dealing with. It must again be stated that a piece of information assigned what might be termed a "bad grade" could still be completely true. If a pathological liar tells you that it's raining, I wouldn't dismiss him despite the rain drops!

Assessing the veracity of Sacred Scripture also puts us face to face with the question of how much we allow our world view to determine what we deem credible. As discussed earlier, intelligence agencies lent credence to "Curveball," because they seem on some level to have allowed their world view, i.e., their assumption that this must be true, to influence their assessment of the information's credibility.

In the Bible, for instance, we have, from time to time, miraculous claims. It goes without saying that someone who believes there is no God and therefore no miracles will dismiss all miraculous claims as being patently false. But it would be bad methodology to then automatically dismiss everything else that is reported in that biblical book as being necessarily false information.

The Historical Reliability of the Torah

The first five books of the Bible, known within the Hebrew Bible as the Torah (Law) are also called the Pentateuch, Greek for "Five Scrolls."

In the book of Genesis, we read an account of the creation of the universe and the world as we know it, with all its various creatures. I do not intend in this book to take on the massive and contentious topic of creationism versus modern conventional science. A statement by His Holiness Kirill, Patriarch of Moscow and All Russia serves to state my personal take on the question of how to interpret the creation narrative:

> We can say that religion, science, and art are different ways of understanding the world and man, the knowledge of the world by man ... Science, for example, answers questions like "how" and "why." Religion - the question "for what." In the center of religious knowledge is the problem of the meaning of life and attitude towards death. ... It is naive to read the book of Genesis as a textbook on the Creation of Man, but it is equally counterproductive to look for the answer to the question of the meaning of life in textbooks on biology or physics.[29]

In other words, I do not feel that a believer is bound to view the book of Genesis literally as a description of Creation. But nor can a Christian view Creation as a random accident. In the

---

[29] http://www.patriarchia.ru/db/text/4579909.html

beginning, God created the heavens and the earth.[30] Science asserts that all the universe as we know it is the result of a Big Bang, in which all matter and energy exploded out of a tiny singular point, but it has no suggestion for how all the matter and energy of the universe could have ever gotten into such a tiny singular point in the first place.

What Genesis Got Right

I do find it intriguing that, while not viewing it as literal history, the Creation Account in Genesis 1 astutely lines up much of cosmological and biological development close to what science thousands of years later also concluded from the astronomical and fossil record. Physicists believe that the very earliest universe was a place devoid of light, since the consolidation of various particles did not yet allow photons to travel freely.[31] And so, for Genesis 1:3 to describe God, after the creation had already begun, declaring, "Let there be light!" is pretty remarkable.

---

[30] Genesis 1:1.

[31] For more details, read the article "First Light and Reionization" on the NASA website. https://jwst.nasa.gov/firstlight.html

We know from paleontology and archaeology that plants emerged on the earth as among the earliest life forms, followed by more complex multi-cellular animals, and that modern humans are one of the final species to appear. This was not obviously apparent to ancient peoples, which makes it so fascinating that the Book of Genesis describes creation in that exact same order.[32]

What Genesis Got Wrong

Now, we need to acknowledge, Genesis also got some things quite wrong. Genesis describes the sun and moon being created after plants had first sprouted.[33] Genesis implies that birds of the sky existed before the land brought forth animals.[34] And so, in the final analysis, the Creation Narrative of the Book of Genesis is not reliable history, as assessed from a scientific standpoint. But believers will certainly take away from reading the first chapter of the Bible that the most important and recurring statement made by God is

---

[32] Plants, Gen 1:11-12; Animals, Gen 1:20-25; Humans, Gen 1:26-27.

[33] Gen 1:14-15.

[34] Gen 1:20.

that "It is good."[35] However God brought the universe into being, it is something glorious we must cherish and nurture.

Independent Confirmation of Biblical Claims

The very oldest thing in the Old Testament that is independently verified would seem to be the existence of a people who called themselves "Israel." The Egyptian Pharaoh Merneptah around 1200 BC recorded in a stone inscription a list of the peoples he had conquered. Included in the list is the following:

Israel is laid waste and his seed is not.

Egyptian hieroglyphs include what are called "determinatives," a series of symbols to tell the reader what a foreign word is, for instance, is it a city or is it a group of people. It is significant that following "Israel" in the stele is the determinative for "people," not "nation."[36] This would seem to

---

[35] Genesis 1:4; 1:10; 1:12; 1:18; 1:21; 1:25; 1:31.

[36] For more details on this inscription, see *Biblical Peoples And Ethnicity: An Archaeological Study of Egyptians, Canaanites, Philistines, And Early Israel 1300-1100 B.C.E.*,

indicate that at this early stage Israel was understood by others and possibly even by themselves to be an ethnic group but not yet a nation state as would seem to be the case by the time of King David.

There also exists independent confirmation for the existence of a man named David who founded a dynasty in Judah. An artifact called the Tel Dan Stele makes reference to the "House of David" (*BTDWD, bayt-Dawid*) and is dated to somewhere between 870 and 750 BC.[37]

King Sennacherib and Jerusalem

There is another event described in the Old Testament, for which there are potentially two non-biblical accounts corroborating in great measure what the Bible says. In approximately 701 BC, the Assyrian King Sennacherib besieged Jerusalem. But he did not conquer it. According to 2 Kings 19:35-36:

---

by Ann E. Killebrew, pp. 154-155 (2005: Society of Biblical Literature Press).

[37] *Beyond the Texts: An Archaeological Portrait of Ancient Israel and Judah*, by William G. Dever, p. 637 (2017: Society of Biblical Literature Press).

And that night [during the siege] the angel of the LORD went forth and slew one hundred and eighty-five thousand in the camp of the Assyrians. And when the men arose early in the morning, behold, these were all dead bodies. Then Sennacherib king of Assyria departed, and went home and dwelt at Nineveh.

Now, it is significant that the biblical account includes a miracle, namely, the intervention of the "angel of the LORD." At face value, if we were rejecting all supernatural claims as therefore non-historical, we would declare immediately that this biblical account is not true. An angel of the LORD, therefore, did no such thing. A hundred and eighty-five thousand soldiers did not die. But would we be justified in reading this account and conclude, because there was the claim of a miracle, that therefore King Sennacherib did not depart? Could we safely conclude, if we reject miracles, that Jerusalem did fall to Sennacherib? Could we go further and conclude that there never was a Kingdom of Judah, or that there never was a Sennacherib, or a city of Jerusalem? Of course not!

It is part of established historical record that Jerusalem did not fall at that time since, after all, it would linger long enough to be conquered by the Babylonians in 587 BC. But what happened in and around Jerusalem in 701 BC was recorded also by the Assyrians themselves. The Annals of Sennacherib are preserved today in three cuneiform artifacts[38] that describe how King Sennacherib went on a campaign westward, including military operations against Egypt and also Judah. It lists a number of cities that the Assyrians besieged. It is very significant that, of all the cities it describes them as attacking, it admits that the Assyrians did not conquer Jerusalem. The Annals state that:

> As for Hezekiah, I shut him up like a caged bird in his royal city of Jerusalem.

What is all the more intriguing is that the Greek historian Herodotus records that, while on this same campaign, the forces of Sennacherib were forced to abandon hostilities against the Egyptians because the various leather accoutrements of their equipment were eaten by a swarm of mice.[39] We know today that mice and rats can carry diseases such as plague, which

---

[38] The account is preserved on cuneiform prisms on display today at the British Museum, the Oriental Institute of Chicago, and the Israel Museum in Jerusalem.

[39] Herodotus, *Histories* 2.141.

certainly is what seems to be described by the sudden and massive loss of life in the Assyrian camp when they were besieging Jerusalem.

Reading between the lines of all three accounts, we can see a unified story. King Sennacherib was forced to abandon his attempt to conquer Jerusalem because of an outbreak of plague among his troops. The inhabitants of Jerusalem saw this as divine intervention, but the fact that they saw it as such does not mean that their report of Sennacherib's withdrawal was a fiction.

In the interest of full disclosure, there are also historical claims made in the Bible that have no corroboration. For instance, the book of Daniel records that a man named Darius the Mede reigned over Babylon between King Belshazzar and Cyrus the Great.[40] But there is no non-biblical corroboration of such a king, despite very extensive record keeping from that time period among the Babylonians.

Assigning a Grade

There is always the possibility that the biblical account is correct and, for whatever reason, the

---

[40] Daniel 5:31.

non-biblical histories are incomplete or even wrong. Even so, using the NATO reliability matrix I presented above, I would assign to the Bible, overall as a literary artifact describing ancient history, a score of B-2:

> **B-Usually reliable**: Minor doubt about authenticity, trustworthiness, or competency; has a history of valid information most of the time.
> **2 - Probably True**: Not confirmed; logical in itself; consistent with other informant on the subject.

I will defend my grade of the Bible in the following way. Number one, even if you believe nothing supernatural, I still assert that the Bible does not engage in a disinformation campaign. In other words, even if the New Testament says that Jesus rose from the dead, but you do not personally believe in the resurrection, there is no reason to believe therefore that there was no such person as Pontius Pilate.[41] The Bible is as reliable a

---

[41] The Roman historian Tacitus, in his work the *Annales* 15.24, describes the crucifixion of Jesus by the Roman Procurator Pontius Pilate. Tacitus wrote his work with access to official governmental annals. He was not quoting the New Testament. In other words, he stands as independent confirmation on the existence of Pontius Pilate and Jesus, and the crucifixion and death of the latter.

source, setting aside supernatural claims, as any other ancient work. The Roman historian Tacitus states that the Emperor Vespasian performed miracles of healing,[42] and yet secular historians are comfortable citing Tacitus as a trusted source for Roman history apart from that claim.

Again, taken as an historical document, I assert that there is no reason to doubt what the Bible says regarding historical personages and events. The fact that the Bible describes miracles is no reason to doubt other assertions. Modern historians cite ancient historians as evidence for reconstructing ancient history all the time, despite supernatural claims being frequently laced within the overall narrative. The Bible should not be given any stricter scrutiny than other ancient works. In Chapter Eight, however, I will again apply the Admiralty Code to a specific claim found in the Bible, the witness testimony of the Apostles that Jesus rose from the dead. And the grade will be very different precisely because it is a supernatural claim.

---

[42] Tacitus, *Historiae* 4.81.

CHAPTER TWO: "HANDING OVER" HUMAN INTELLIGENCE

As discussed in the previous chapter, HUMINT studies the information that one person usually willingly gives to another person. This is different from Signals Intelligence, which we will explore in the next chapter, in which the information is ordinarily intercepted electronically without the two parties in the exchange knowing that someone else "eavesdropped" on the conversation. In HUMINT, information is knowingly and willingly "*handed over*" to another person.

This makes the lens of HUMINT particularly important to study key information from the New Testament in particular, because the operative verb in the New Testament which describes the transmission of the very Gospel message itself is the Greek verb *paradidomi* (past tense, *paredoka*), "to hand over."[43]

Note this verse from St. Paul's 1st Letter to the Corinthians which shows how this verb is used:

> For I received from the Lord what I also handed over/delivered (*paredoka*) to you, that the Lord Jesus, on the night when he was handed over/betrayed (*paredideto*), took bread...[44]

You'll see here that the verb, which in its root simply means, "to hand over," can have a neutral meaning (to deliver) but also the negative connotation of "to give something (or someone) over with ill intent (to betray)."

"Handing Over" the Faith

St. Paul later in this epistle again uses this same verb to describe the transmission of the Gospel message:

---

[43] I will provide transliteration of the original languages only when necessary to highlight the importance of the use of a word or phrase.

[44] 1 Corinthians 11:23.

> For I handed over (*paredoka*) unto you first of all what I also received —that our Lord Jesus Christ died for our sins according to the Scriptures.[45]

Note some other important examples:

> Thanks be to God that you who once were slaves of sin now have become obedient from the heart to the type of doctrine you were delivered (*paredothete*).[46]

> Contend for the Faith, which was once for all handed over (*paradotheise*) to the Saints.[47]

These last two examples clearly state that it is not isolated teachings where are "handed over" to the Church. The *entirety* of the Gospel message, THE FAITH itself, with the body of its doctrine, has been *handed over* to the Church.

And so a crucial question that now must be asked is, "Where does all of this teaching that was handed over reside?" Take a look at the King James Version of a verse from 1st Corinthians in

---

[45] 1 Corinthians 15:3.

[46] Romans 6:17.

[47] Jude 1:3.

which St. Paul once again uses the verb *paradidomi* to describe "handing over" Gospel teaching:

> Now I praise you, brethren, that ye remember me in all things, and keep the **ordinances**, as I handed them over (*paredoka*) to you.[48]

Merriam-Webster's Dictionary defines **ordinance** as "an authoritative decree or law."[49] Based on this translation, we would expect that the Greek word thus translated would come from a root meaning "to order" or the like.

Instead, the word here translated as "ordinances" is *paradoseis*. If you've been paying attention to the multiple cases of the verb "to hand over" (*paradidomi*), you might realize that the noun here is derived from that same verb!

In other words, this noun actually means "things handed over." A translation that preserves the Greek text of 1 Cor 11:2 better would be:

> Keep the *things handed over*, as I handed them over to you.

---

[48] 1 Corinthians 11:2.

[49] P. 508, *Merriam-Webster Dictionary* (2016 Edition: Merriam Webster, Inc.).

What exactly are these "things handed over" and where can we find them that we may hold fast to them today?

And why does the King James Bible translate a word that means "things handed over" as "ordinance," thereby obscuring from our eyes the connection between the noun and the verb so important in describing the transmission of the Gospel itself?

To get the answer, let's look at another verse in the New Testament that contains the noun *paradosis*, "thing handed over."

Note the following:

So then, brothers, stand fast and hold firm to the "things handed over" (*paradoseis*) which you were taught, whether by our spoken word or by our letter.[50]

Was it All "Handed Over" Into the Bible?

St. Paul tells us that these things handed over are things that he himself had written or that he had told them orally when he was with them.

---

[50] 2 Thessalonians 2:15.

Here is where someone might reasonably assert that all those things which have been "handed over" to the Church to believe as the body of Christian faith must be contained in the Bible. And, if that is true, we should believe what is in the Bible and, as regards Christian doctrine, we should not believe anything not found in the Bible.

Such a teaching was the driving force of the Protestant Reformation which began at the end of the 16th century AD. It is called in Latin (the theological language of the day) *Sola Scriptura*, "The Bible Alone."

One problem with that belief is that the Bible itself says otherwise:

> But there are also many other things which Jesus did. Were every one of them to be written down, I suppose that the world itself could not contain the books that would be written.[51]

Granted, St. John is engaging in a bit of exaggeration here, but the point must still be taken that, if the whole world could not contain all Jesus did, then certainly the Bible as we know it also does *not* contain it.

---

[51] John 21:25.

What St. Paul wrote to the Thessalonians above also rules out the notion that all of what was "handed over," either by his spoken word or by his letter, is contained in the Bible. The New Testament is a finite piece of literature. It is four gospels, the book of Acts, an assortment of his letters, an assortment of letters written by others, and one Apocalypse. It is disingenuous to interpret what he wrote as meaning "hold fast to the things handed over, whether eventually recorded in other books of the New Testament or in my Epistles eventually included in the New Testament."

To read 2 Thess 2:15 at face value, St. Paul is anxious that the Christians in that city hold fast to the body of Christian belief and practice, which he knows is valid and genuine, regardless of whether it has been handed over in oral or written form.

"Handing Over" Traditions

I've been purposely avoiding until now discussing the best translation of the word *paradosis*. It does indeed by its derivation mean "thing handed over." But we have in English a word derived from the Latin verb also meaning "to hand over." That verb, *tradere*, gives us the Latin word *traditio*. The English borrowing is *tradition*.

That is exactly what a tradition is. Perhaps in your family there was some practice, and no one even remembers how or when it got started, but you perpetuate it year after year. It was something that you have handed down, or handed over generation after generation. And you may lovingly cherish these "family traditions" and faithfully pass them on, intending thereby to enrich the next generation.

Nevertheless, when it comes to Christianity, many Protestants have been taught that tradition is bad. They have been taught that much of what Catholics (and Orthodox, as well) believe and practice that is not found in the Bible is "just human tradition" and therefore not just *non-biblical*. They are taught that it is *anti-biblical*.

And I guess that might have been why the translator of the King James Bible used the word *ordinance*. Since St. Paul was commending those particular "things handed over," the translator felt uncomfortable translating the word as *traditions*, since his faith community believes that *traditions* are anti-biblical.

In Chapter Six I will go into more depth on the overall issue of biblical translations. This example is emblematic of the fact that translations are also simultaneously interpretations of the Bible, sometimes intentionally obscuring the original text from the reader.

Are Traditions All Bad?

This attitude stems from exactly one passage of the New Testament, parallel versions of the same passage found in both Mark 7 and Matthew 15. In this passage, Jesus condemns those who follow *human* traditions rather than following the Law. What is important to note in this passage is that Jesus does not actually condemn tradition or traditions as such. He condemns traditions that are explicitly described as being of *non-divine* origin. Everywhere you see the word "tradition" underlined in this passage is the Greek word *paradosis*, the same thing that St. Paul tells us to hold fast to. But I will also upper case and bold the source of the traditions Jesus condemns here:

> Then Pharisees and scribes came to Jesus from Jerusalem and said, "Why do your disciples transgress the tradition **OF THE ELDERS**? For they do not wash their hands when they eat." He answered them, "And why do you transgress the commandment of God for the sake of **YOUR** tradition? For God commanded, 'Honor your father and your mother', and 'He who speaks evil of father

or mother, let him surely die'. But you say, 'If anyone tells his father or his mother, What you would have gained from me is given to God, he need not honor his father'. So, for the sake of **YOUR** <u>tradition</u>, you have made void the word of God.[52]

As the passage continues in Matt 15:9 (and in Mark 7:7), Jesus condemns these Pharisees and scribes and their adherence to purely human traditions by quoting a passage from Isaiah 29:13:

In vain do they worship me, teaching as doctrines the precepts of men.

But what is utterly fascinating here is that the quote Mark puts in Jesus' mouth is from the Greek translation of the Hebrew Bible known as the Septuagint (LXX). And that Greek translation does indeed match the sentiment of condemning human tradition. But the Hebrew original of Isaiah 29:13 does not serve the argument nearly as well as the Greek. Here is a literal translation of the Hebrew:

---

[52] Matthew 15:1-6 (Mark 7:1-13).

And their fear of me is learned as a human commandment.

Some Protestant Christians have unfortunately quoted this whole passage as an automatic condemnation of all extra-biblical traditions as being necessarily against the Will of God. Here's why that cannot be true:

1) As studied above, St. Paul and others describe the Gospel message itself as a *tradition*, to be accepted whether in written or oral form.
2) In the very passage so often cited as condemning tradition (Matthew 15:1-6 above), the argument quotes a *human* translation that better makes the point than the Hebrew original text.
3) Finally, the Bible does not even always condemn human tradition as necessarily bad. In Jeremiah 35:18-19, for instance, God praises the Rechabites for faithfully maintaining what he explicitly describes as a commandment of their ancestor Jonadab.

The ultimate question is not whether those non-biblical things that Catholics and Orthodox Christians do and teach are *traditions*. The issue is whether they are purely human traditions or are instead part of those things "things handed down" by the Apostles, but just did not get recorded in the New Testament.

In the next two chapters we will explore more deeply how to best understand the text of the Bible through the lens of intelligence analysis. And we will then see whether some of these "non-biblical traditions" might just be found in the Bible after all.

Chapter Three: Signals Intelligence (SIGINT)

Definition of SIGINT

Signals Intelligence (SIGINT) involves the interception of electronic signals. Within the intelligence community, intercepted signals that involve communication are called COMINT (Communications Intelligence). Signals of more technical data are called ELINT (Electronic Intelligence).

But since the vast majority of Signals Intelligence sent to US policy makers is, technically, COMINT, people frequently just use the term SIGINT to mean personal communications as well. And that's the term I will use.

Who Conducts SIGINT?

The US Agency tasked with conducting SIGINT is the National Security Agency, which is an entity within the Department of Defense. This agency was created in 1952 by a memorandum issued by President Truman. The impetus was the realization that the military and the CIA were wasting US resources by jointly targeting the same adversaries by SIGINT. So the very intelligent decision was reached that SIGINT should be conducted by only one organization and so a joint civilian/military agency was created.

Because the memo creating the NSA was itself a classified document, the very existence of the NSA was a secret for many years. This gave rise to the joke that NSA stood for "No Such Agency."

What are the most important issues in SIGINT?

Unlike HUMINT, in which we receive information we know the source wanted us to have, information obtained by SIGINT is assumed to be something the source did not think we were "listening in on."

As such, it has an automatic degree of

reliability, provided we are interpreting it correctly. And therein lies the real challenge with SIGINT.

Imagine the last email you sent to a very close friend. You referred to things you and your friend know well. Maybe you made inside jokes, based on anecdotes going all the way back to high school!

Now imagine some Russian SIGINT agent somewhere managed to intercept that email. (And I hope the Russians do not have that capability!) First off, if she does not know English very well, she cannot make any sense of your email. But the Russians can probably hire competent linguists.

Even if you used well-known English words, you may have been using them to refer to things which, not knowing the background context, would make no sense to another person. In other words, you can say something to a friend, knowing that the friend will successfully "read between the lines," but that Russian SIGINT agent will report that she knows all the words and simply does not understand what the letter is really saying.

And if you used very vernacular slang in your email, she may run into trouble for other reasons. This Russian agent could have learned English starting in middle school. She might have majored in English in college. She may speak it excellently, with just the tiniest hint of an accent.

But she still cannot completely understand your email. Why? Because there are things that only a full native speaker, growing up in the country in question, will be able to hear or read and understand.

How do I know she does not understand your email? Because I, with a PhD and years of Arabic study, regularly faced things at the NSA that I could not understand. Don't get me wrong. I spent my entire day translating things well. I was promoted to GS-13 because of my skills. But there were regularly things I could not interpret because I am not a native speaker of Arabic. But luckily, that did not mean that crucial intelligence at the NSA could not be processed.

Let me assure you, dear reader, that working at the NSA are patriotic Americans of virtually every original nationality. I worked with women and men from every country of the Middle East. They became US Citizens and they offer their linguistic skills to the defense of our nation. And we should be grateful to them for their service. I am particularly grateful to them because, on many occasions, as a non-native speaker of Arabic, I needed their expertise to solve particularly difficult puzzles for our national security.

Lessons Learned

When you see or hear a communication sent from one person to another, there are numerous interpretive issues you need to consider. You may overhear an exchange that will only make sense if you are fully immersed in the culture of those involved. You may also hear only one side of a conversation. You could assume what the other side is saying and be completely wrong or completely right. Imagine the following brief exchange you could overhear. If all you heard was the B side, you would have to engage in speculation as to what the B side was responding to:

[A) When is the Wedding?]
B) At 9AM.
[A) Is it an open bar at the reception?]
B) It is.

[A) When is the attack?]
B) At 9AM.
[A) Is the bomb ready?]
B) It is.

Now, add in the possibility that the term "Wedding" could be a known cover term for

"Attack" and "Open Bar" could mean "weapons ready" and you can begin to understand just how hard it is to interpret intelligence from within SIGINT.

In general, the implication of SIGINT is that great care must be taken when interpreting any information you receive. That is the same whether you are one of the intended recipients of the communication or whether you simply overhear a communication somehow. We must never forget the real possibility of a misunderstanding in either case.

Applications for Understanding the Bible

If the primary challenge of SIGINT is understanding a message with no further context than the message itself, SIGINT issues would seem to most directly concern how we approach reading the Epistles of the New Testament. In a very real sense, we have them as if they were intercepted messages. St. Paul and others wrote letters to churches and individuals. In the case of a letter sent to a whole church, the authors certainly did intend a large number of people to receive the message they were sending.

Because the author of the letter had been one of their cherished apostles, they read it publicly. They reread it to the congregation at intervals. They made copies of it and sent it to other local churches, so even more people could be edified by the message. And some of what the message contains is clear to any reader, especially those who already know some of the background information being discussed.

It would occasionally happen at the NSA that, if a piece of traffic was not clear, an attempt would be made to obtain, either through open source investigation or additional tasking, information that might better explain the unclear part of a previous intercept. We do something similar in biblical studies. If we are uncertain what a Greek or Hebrew word means, the best way to understand it is to see if that same word occurs in that same author, but in a context that better explains it. Next best would be to see if that word occurs in another New Testament book. But if a Greek word or grammatical construction is not found anywhere else in the Bible, we certainly do consider as valuable the use of that word by Greek authors outside the biblical canon. And when we do not understand a word in Hebrew, we resort to related languages, such as Arabic, for an idea of what that word might mean.

It is worth nothing that any admission that information outside the Bible may be valuable in better understanding the biblical text is proof that the Bible requires external confirmation to be properly interpreted. The desire to get at the ultimate truth of the Bible naturally wants to pull in whatever information is necessary, whether this is the meaning of a word in a related language or the use of a key phrase in an extra-biblical book.

Because SIGINT, more so than HUMINT, is concerned with the accurate translation of language, SIGINT issues ultimately apply not just to "intercepted letters" like the works of St. Paul, but to the totality of Scripture. The challenge for the interpreter, regardless of the biblical period or genre, is that we lack both the perfect linguistic skills but also the context to completely understand everything in the transmission.

Getting to the Truth

One way that intelligence analysis differs significantly from modern literary study, including some strains of modern biblical criticism, is that intelligence analysis hinges on determining what is *actually* true. You might find it confusing to hear me say that modern biblical criticism is not always concerned with what is true. And so let me clarify what I mean.

In most cases, when a human spy gives information to another, the message itself is relatively clear. The only lingering question is whether that message is worthy of belief. In SIGINT, there might from time to time be confusion about what the communication means on a linguistic level. Or there might be confusion about what exactly was meant because of a lack of context. But the real issue, the only thing that gives us anything of intelligence value, is figuring out what the person who produced this message actually meant by it.

Theoretically all of the various forms of biblical criticism are employed (or should be) to arrive at the same result. But there are branches of literary and biblical criticism which do something different. Canonical criticism seeks to understand the text in its final form as a text of meaning for a specific community. In that sense, what the original writer meant could be less important than how a community uses the text. Also, in the wider field of literary study, there is an array of approaches known as "New Criticism" which largely reject the primacy of author intent so crucial in the area of intelligence analysis.

A Hypothetical Test Case

To recap, the SIGINT analyst needs to arrive at as complete an understanding as possible of what exactly the originator of the message actually meant by it, and also the significance of all the content of the message within the context that created it. Let's explore these issues in the following fictional example message we hypothetically intercepted from a (wanted) young man:

> Tomorrow I'm gonna go at noon to eat at the best pizzeria in town!

If, hypothetically, the person that said this message is someone that law enforcement would very much like to arrest, this could be a crucial piece of Intel. And so, we hand it off to the analyst. The first thing is that, as long as the analyst is a native speaker of English, they are going to automatically know that "gonna" is just rapidly spoken speech for "going to." And the rest of the message is linguistically very straightforward. However, to arrest this wanted individual we are going to then need to know two more facts:

A) What town is he talking about?
B) What's the best pizzeria in that town?

Without going into classified details, it may be possible to make a very educated guess on the intended town based on other information collected in the SIGINT process. It may also be that the intended town showed up openly in other communications.

To use a biblical example, if St. Paul in one intercepted communication made a reference to his "home town," the fact that other communications refer to him by his original name as "Saul of Tarsus" would let us confidently know what home town he was talking about.

So let's assume that, for various reasons, we are confident we know what town he is referring to. Much trickier is going to be determining the intended reference for B above, "What's the best pizzeria in that town?" First off, it is not impossible that the originator of the message is expressing something that is purely his opinion. Even so, we have to try to catch this guy. And that means at least trying to determine the restaurant he is probably talking about.

So we use social media and we learn that 99% of the people in this area believe that the best such joint in town is "Isabella's Pizzeria" on the north side. The other 1% spread their votes over a dozen or so other establishments. If we have the resources to send officers to attempt an arrest at only one site, it would be mindless to not send them to Isabella's, right? Because in all likelihood, he is one of the 99%, not one of the 1%. And so we send the team to Isabella's fully knowing that there still is a chance, however small, that we are wrong.

And the extraction team arrives at Isabella's and our target never shows up. As unlikely as it was, he was a member of the 1%. So, the information we got from that message ceases to be what, in the business, we call "actionable intelligence."

But even as the moment has passed, it will always remain true that the originator of the message did mean *something* by "best pizzeria in town." The fact that we cannot figure out what the message entirely means does not change that fact. And the fact that this information has ceased to matter for catching him this afternoon does not change the fact that he meant *something* when he said it.

Finally Learning the Truth

So let's imagine that young man eludes the law and goes on to lead a quiet life somewhere. And let's imagine that twenty years later he fathers a child. His daughter grows up, and from time to time her father tells her about his life back in his hometown. In the course of time he passes away, but his daughter thrives. She has a family and let's imagine at age 80, her great grandson, who is creating a family history, asks her, "What can you tell me about your father?"

She smiles and says, "Well, he always talked about how his favorite restaurant in the world when he was a young man was this little hole-in-the-wall place called 'Johnnie's Pizzeria', on the east side of town."

So, armed with this testimony, do we now likely know where he actually went to lunch that day? It would seem, in all probability, yes. The information she provided to her great-grandson is reliable. It came directly from a source who would have no credible reason to mislead his daughter about this piece of nostalgia.

And yet, note that in the timeline I have presented, this information is one hundred years old from the date of the lunch. And yet it is undeniably an important piece of cultural information which, having been passed down in the family, helps to explain an obscure linguistic communication from long ago.

Implications for Traditions Outside the Bible

Just as I described earlier regarding the use of other texts and ultimately even other languages to understand an obscure linguistic point, it is evident that a piece of cultural information passed down through even lengthy periods of time could be crucial to understanding an obscure passage of Scripture.

A belief or practice first attested in the year AD 200 was probably not invented in the year 199. If that belief or practice, first attested in AD 200 was not accompanied by a backlash from other parts of the community, it becomes more likely that it was already a well-ingrained practice of the community.

An application of both the HUMINT model on tradition and the SIGINT model on Scripture would come to the conclusion that there could be evidence in Scripture for a later openly attested belief or practice which would only be noticed if we accept that tradition preserves the beliefs and practices of the earlier community.

The community which preserved and meticulously copied by hand manuscripts of the Bible could not have been believing and practicing things that were contrary to the Scriptures. Consider how frankly bizarre it would be for a community with beliefs and practices which were actually repugnant to its own collection of Scriptures to then faithfully pass on those same Scriptures through considerable time, cost, and energy for 1500 years.

To use an analogy, it would be like a criminal doing a horrible job of not cleaning up the crime scene. If the community of the Church handed down those Scriptures, it was only because that community understood those sacred texts to be in accord with their beliefs. And if we find that the community holds firm beliefs in things not found explicitly in those texts, it can only mean that the community that faithfully passed on those Scriptures did not in any way believe that there was any inconsistency in that. It can only mean that the community believed it was perfectly fine to believe things not found at all in their own sacred writings.

Making Sense out of a Garbled Text

It is a reality that, despite how good our intelligence gathering might be, from time to time various factors may result in the product of our intercepted message containing what can only be described as a "garble." We had a joke at the NSA that Murphy's Law of Garbles is that if there was to be only one garble in an intercept, it somehow managed to occur right in the middle of the most important and intelligence worthy part of the intercept.

There are many places in the Bible where the passage of time and the imperfect nature of human copying have resulted in a "garble" in Sacred Scripture.

Here is an interesting example of how this sometimes occurred. In the book of Deuteronomy 31:1, the Hebrew text passed down in what we call the MT reads as follows:

And Moses went and spoke.
wylk mšh wy'mr

The Greek Translation (LXX), however, reads differently:

And Moses finished speaking.
kai synetelesen mouses lalon

It would seem that the Hebrew text that the Greek translator was looking at was different from the MT. In fact, it was almost identical, but it had two letters inverted:

MT: *wylk*
LXX: *wykl*

So, one of these is a typo and one of them is the original reading. A fragment of Jeremiah 31:1 found among the Dead Sea Scrolls contains the same reading as the LXX, confirming the fact that such a variant really did exist in Hebrew.[53] Interestingly, the same "typo" occurs in the opposite direction in Joshua 19:49:

Masoretic Test
And they finished...
[*wyklw*]

LXX
And they went
kai eporeuthesan [*wylkw*]

---

[53] 1Q5 (fragment 13,2, 1.4).

Each and every case of such "typos" in transmission needs to be independently studied and assessed to arrive at the best guess as to what the original text really w as. But if you think about it, the very fact that the text of the Bible, passed down for centuries through hand-written copies, could therefore contain such mistakes, should tell us that basing our faith on the precise text of the Bible is impossible.

Even if no crucial point of doctrine hinges on choosing the right version in the case of a known typo, even so, it remains entirely possible that some point of doctrine could be based on a text that is, in fact, an *unknown typo*. It could be that this particular typo happened so early in the transmission of the text that no alternative reading exists to tell us that it is a typo at all.

In other words, if there is even one typo in the text that we know of, there must be many others about which we know not. It would, therefore, be much safer to base our faith on the traditions of the community than on the precise text of the Bible that the community painstakingly, but imperfectly, passed down to us.

Chapter Four: Putting HUMINT and SIGINT Together to Better Understand the Bible

HUMINT, as we explored, is assessed based on the reliability of the source and the credibility of the information provided. SIGINT, on the other hand, is assessed primarily on the importance of the information, but practically on the accuracy of its translation and then on its proper interpretation based on whatever context is available.

Policy makers who are consumers of the product of the various intelligence agencies are always especially gratified when some important point is truly and independently verified in both HUMINT and SIGINT. A single HUMINT source can be a liar. A single SIGINT intercept can be misinterpreted. But when something can be confirmed with both intelligence disciplines, we arrive at a greater confidence that we know the truth. And remember, our Lord told us that knowing the truth is his will for us. For he said, "you shall know the truth and the truth will set you free."[54]

In this chapter I will explore as a case study for the fusion of HUMINT and SIGINT a doctrine that currently divides Protestants from Catholics (Roman Catholic and Orthodox). Starting in the 16th century AD and continuing to the current day, there were a number of practices and doctrines accepted by the Catholic and Orthodox Churches but which have been rejected by various Protestant bodies on the basis that they were not sufficiently endorsed by Scripture. As described above, the handing down of such things is most effectively studied through the paradigm of HUMINT, in order to assess its reliability and credibility. And while their authenticity as early Christian belief and practice can be examined through HUMINT, a further verification of such things through SIGINT, i.e. an expression of them somewhere in

---

[54] John 8:32.

Scripture, would serve not only as an endorsement of the HUMINT reliability, but as the evidence Protestants might need to, if not accept such practices, at least not view them as utterly contrary to Christian belief and practice.

I will focus on a doctrine that, arguably, was the most repugnant of all the Catholic/Orthodox beliefs and practices to the first generation of Protestant reformers—the concept that the Eucharist is a sacrifice. As I stated earlier, it is my firm belief that viewing the Bible through the lens of Intelligence Analysis can build bridges between the different Christian communities. If these methods can foster understanding on such a contentious issue as this, it will certainly be a fruitful endeavor.

The Eucharist as a Sacrifice

Setting aside momentarily exactly what kind of sacrifice different churches might think the Eucharist is, there is no doubt that the Catholic and Orthodox Churches both believe it is a sacrifice and openly speak of it as such. So, for instance, as a priest during the Divine Eucharistic Liturgy, I pray the following:

Accept our supplications, O God; make us worthy **to offer** unto thee prayers and supplications, and **unbloody sacrifices** for all thy people.

And later:

And graciously grant us to obtain grace in thy sight, that **our sacrifice** may be acceptable unto thee; and that the good spirit of thy grace may rest upon us, and upon **these Holy Gifts, now offered up** unto thee, and upon all thy people.

In the Catholic Mass, the people say the following, directed at the priest:

May the Lord accept **the sacrifice at your hands**, for the praise and glory of his name, for our good and for the good of all his holy Church.

Then, soon after, the priest prays:

To you, therefore, most merciful Father, we make humble prayer and petition through Christ, your Son, our Lord, that you accept and bless these gifts, **these offerings**, **these holy and unblemished sacrifices**...

In contrast to this, Martin Luther wrote the following, rejecting the notion that the Eucharist is, in any way, a sacrifice. He admits in this passage that the idea of the Eucharist as a sacrifice is both widespread and appears early in Church history, but he rejects it on the grounds that the Bible does not include *any* reference to it:

> It is the common belief that the **mass is a sacrifice**, which is **offered to God**. Even the words of the canon seem to imply this, when they speak of "these gifts, these presents, **these holy sacrifices**..." [55]

So Luther openly admits that the Eucharist as a sacrifice is a common belief, and it is one that the prayers of the Liturgy clearly state. He continues:

> Added to these are the **sayings of the holy fathers, the great number of examples, and the widespread practice uniformly observed throughout the world**.

Luther admits that the earliest Christian writers, whose works he has read, also believe in the doctrine of the Eucharist as a sacrifice. So why would he reject this doctrine so strongly? He explains as follows:

---

[55] Martin Luther, *Babylonian Captivity of the Church* (1520).

Over against all these things, firmly entrenched as they are, we must resolutely set the words and example of Christ. For unless we firmly hold that the mass is the promise and testament of Christ, as the words clearly say: we shall lose the whole gospel and all its comfort. **Let us permit nothing to prevail against these words**-even though an angel from heaven should teach otherwise [Gal. 1:8]-**for [the words of Jesus] CONTAIN NOTHING ABOUT A WORK OR A SACRIFICE** (emphasis my own).

While it is true that ecumenists have tried to assert that Luther was primarily reacting to gross excesses of his day, it remains true that the Protestant churches today do not, as Catholic and Orthodox do, openly call the Eucharist a sacrifice, stemming primarily from Luther and others not seeing such a doctrine clearly expressed in Scripture.

Studying the Problem through Intelligence Analysis

It has been said that 9/11 was an intelligence failure stemming in part from the inability of the various branches of the intelligence community to share with one another pieces of the puzzle that they each had.[56] In other words, one intelligence agency may have collected information but simply did not fully understood its significance, since they did not have the necessary other piece of the puzzle to make sense of their information. In the wake of that disaster, the previous paradigm, in which information was always on a "NEED TO KNOW" basis, was replaced with a new collaborative methodology—"RESPONSIBILITY TO SHARE."[57]

I will show that Luther's rejection of the belief in the Eucharist as a sacrifice is best viewed through the paradigm of an intelligence failure. I will show that, while he perhaps was acting in good faith, he lacked a key piece of the puzzle that could have convinced him of the truth of this doctrine.

Luther above freely admits that the belief in the Eucharist as a sacrifice was early and widespread. But he states that none of that matters, since the

---

[56] "9/11 Congressional Report Faults F.B.I.-C.I.A. Lapses." https://www.nytimes.com/2003/07/24/us/9-11-congressional-report-faults-fbi-cia-lapses.html

[57] "How 9/11 Transformed the Intelligence Community." https://www.wsj.com/articles/SB10001424053111904537404576554430822300352

words of Jesus "contain nothing about a work or a sacrifice."

Now, Luther builds his entire Gospel focus of "Salvation by Faith Alone" from the Epistles of St. Paul, not the words of Jesus,[58] so Luther presumably would or at least certainly *should* be very interested in whether St. Paul anywhere seems to describe the Eucharist as a sacrifice. I will show you now that St. Paul certainly did so. In fact, I will show you that four different verses in 1 Corinthians teach the doctrine that the Eucharist is a sacrifice.

#1: St. Paul Compares the Eucharist to Two Other Sacrifices

In 1 Cor 10:14-21, St. Paul discusses the controversy of whether a Christian can eat meat which has been sacrificed to idols. In ancient times, temples sold excess meat left over after

---

[58] Indeed, salvation by faith alone runs not only contrary to Jesus' Parable of the Sheep and the Goats (Matt 25:31-46), but is even countered by St. Paul himself, who writes in Romans 2:6 that God will render to each "according to his works." And we must not forget that Sacred Scripture records St. James as writing "You see that a man is justified by works and not by faith alone" (James 2:24). Perhaps theologians can find clever ways to pretend there is no inconsistency here. Intelligence analysts certainly cannot.

sacrifices, essentially functioning as meat markets for the people. And so, for early Christians, the question arose as to whether a Christian, who does not believe in the pagan gods to which that meat was sacrificed, could morally buy and eat that product. St. Paul in this passage says they cannot, arguing, in fact, that such meat was actually sacrificed to demons. And the main point he makes is that Christians need to chose where they have their "participation" or "communion" (Greek: *koinonia*):

> Therefore, my beloved, shun the worship of idols. I speak as to sensible men; judge for yourselves what I say.
> **The cup of blessing which we bless, is it not a participation (*koinonia*) in the blood of Christ? The bread which we bread, is it not a participation (*koinonia*) in the body of Christ?**
> Because there is one bread, we who are many are one body, for we all partake of the one bread.
> **Consider the people of Israel; are not those who eat the sacrifices participators (*koinonoi*) in the altar?**
> What do I imply then? That food offered to idols is anything, or that an idol is anything?
> No, I imply that what pagans sacrifice, they offer to demons, and not to God. **I do not want you to be**

> **participators (*koinonous*) with demons.**
> **You cannot drink of the cup of the Lord and the cup of demons.**
> **You cannot partake of the table of the Lord (*trapezes kuriou*) and the table of demons.**[59]

You will notice that in this passage, St. Paul uses forms of the same root word (*koinon-*) meaning "participation" or "participators" in three contexts:

1) The Eucharist
2) Sacrifices made in the Temple in Jerusalem
3) Sacrifices made to demons (pagan gods)

He clearly, therefore, considers these three things to be analogous to each other. So even if he does not explicitly state here, "The Eucharist is a sacrifice," he does believe that, on some level, it is like these other two sacrifices in some significant way.

---

[59] 1 Cor 10:14-21.

#2: Jesus Himself Calls the Eucharist a Sacrifice

Martin Luther had said that the words of Jesus "contain nothing about a work or a sacrifice."

Jesus says, while instituting the Eucharist, that we are to "Do this in remembrance of me."[60] If you ask most people what that even means, they will likely say things along the line of "Remember all Jesus did or represented when we celebrate Communion."

But what are the original words Jesus used? And might they include a reference to another biblical passage? Jesus' original Aramaic words here have not been preserved in Sacred Scripture. But the Greek of the passage here and in the Synoptic Gospels contains a phrase that has exactly one parallel elsewhere in Scripture:

>...in remembrance of me
>*eis ten emen anamnesin*[61]

Compare this to the LXX translation of Leviticus 24:7, in a discussion of a sacrifice of

---

[60] 1 Cor 11:24-25.

[61] 1 Cor 11:24.

incense and bread:

> And you shall put pure frankincense with each row, **that it may go with the bread as a memorial offering (*eis anamnesin*)** to be offered by fire to the LORD.

There is no other place in the LXX where the noun *anamnesin* is governed by the preposition *eis*. This is, therefore, a clear allusion by Jesus to the passage from Leviticus.

If you translate the noun *anamnesin* in 1 Corinthians as it is rendered in Leviticus, this ceases to be just a fond thought about remembering Jesus. Instead, this is Jesus himself describing this ritual involving bread and wine with an allusion to an Old Testament bread offering:

> Do this as a memorial offering of me.

And so, St. Paul compares the Eucharist to two other sacrifices, strongly implying that the Eucharist is one as well. Jesus himself, in the words instituting the Eucharist, calls the Eucharist a Memorial Sacrifice. This would be enough to at least establish that belief in the Eucharist as a sacrifice is not repugnant to Christian faith.

#3: St. Paul Implies that the Eucharist is a Sacrifice

Later in that same passage, St. Paul writes the following about the Eucharist:

> For as often as you eat this bread and drink this cup, you proclaim (*katangellete*) the Lord's death until he comes.[62]

The verb here translated (*katangellein*) can indeed mean "to proclaim" in a generic sense of just to proclaim some information to another person. That is how it is used, for instance in Romans 1:8:

> First, I thank my God through Jesus Christ for you all, because your faith is being proclaimed (*katangelletai*) through all the world.

But the verb can also be used in what linguists call a "performative" sense. In other words, you do not just "proclaim" a fact, but the very act of "proclaiming" makes something become a reality. For instance, note the following usage in a non-biblical Greek passage:

---

[62] 1 Cor 11:26.

> [These men] have declared war (*polemon katengelkasin*) instead of peace.[63]

When you "declare war," you create the state of war by the very proclamation.

I would suggest that St. Paul could be using the verb in a similar sense in 1 Cor 11:26. If St. Paul were stating that the act of celebrating the Eucharist is somehow merely a proclamation that Jesus died, the ritual would seem somewhat pointless, and certainly something inconceivable for Jesus to have instituted. Instead, using a performative sense of the verb, St. Paul is teaching that, in the act of the Eucharist, the very death of Jesus is somehow made present in a mystical sense. It is "declared" into the present sacramental moment, just as declaring war makes war real and present.

This is precisely how the *Catechism of the Catholic Church* (*CCC*) describes the Eucharist:

---

[63] *Lysias* 25.30.

The Eucharist is thus a sacrifice because it *re-presents* (makes present) the sacrifice of the cross.[64]

One of the biggest misunderstandings Protestants have about Catholic and Orthodox teaching on this point is the notion that we believe we are somehow "re-sacrificing" Jesus. The very reason we call it the "unbloody" sacrifice is because we certainly do not believe Jesus is sacrificed again in the Holy Eucharist. Rather, our earthly sacrifice of bread and wine, through the power of the Holy Spirit, mystically makes present the death of Jesus.[65]

#4: St. Paul Again Describes the Eucharist as a Sacrifice

For the fourth and final and ultimately most important proof that St. Paul believed the Eucharist was a sacrifice, we return to his discussion of the Eucharist in chapter 10 of 1st

---

[64] *CCC* 1366. While I am not a Roman Catholic, this statement serves to express the mystery of the Eucharistic Sacrifice nicely.

[65] The sacrifice of Christ and the sacrifice of the Eucharist are *one single sacrifice*: (*CCC* 1367).

Corinthians. As I described above, St. Paul stated that Christians have their "participation" (*koinonia*) in the Eucharist and not in the sacrifices in the Pagan and Jerusalem Temple and where others are participators (*koinonoi*). He stated that Christians cannot partake of both the "table of the Lord" (*trapezes kuriou*) and the table of demons.

This phrase "table of the Lord" is naturally understood by Christian readers as a synonym for "Communion" or "Eucharist." But what if it is actually a quote from the Old Testament? What if it is a quote from the Old Testament that many other early Christian writers knew was a reference to the Eucharist as a sacrifice?

Remember that Martin Luther admitted that belief in the Eucharist as a sacrifice was both ancient and widespread. He did not care, because he did not believe the doctrine was present in the New Testament. I believe that what I have demonstrated thus far already proves him very wrong.

As an example of what Luther admitted existed in the writings of the Early Church, note St. Ignatius of Antioch, writing to the Philadelphians, somewhere around the year AD 110:

Be careful therefore to observe one Eucharist. For there is one flesh of our Lord Jesus Christ and one cup unto union in his blood. There is one sacrificial altar (*thusiasterion*).[66]

A passage such as this is precisely what Martin Luther was referring to when he admitted that the belief was ancient. There is an even earlier extra-biblical reference to the Eucharist as sacrifice that Luther never saw. And this is because it is found in a very early Christian work known as the Didache (Teaching of the Apostles). Scholars estimate that it comes from the late 1st century AD, that is to say, it was written at a time when many Christians would have learned their Christianity from the Apostles themselves. Although the Didache was known and quoted by early Christian writers, the actual work itself was lost and would have unfortunately been unavailable to Martin Luther when he was active. The Didache was rediscovered in an ancient manuscript in 1874 in Istanbul and is now acknowledged by scholars to be a window into the communal life of a Christian community in the late 1st century AD.

---

[66] Ignatius of Antioch, *To the Philadelphians* 4.

The Didache Holds the Key

Regarding the Eucharist, the Didache states:

> And **on the Lord's own day** gather yourselves together and **break bread and give thanks**, first confessing your transgressions, **that your sacrifice may be pure**. ... for **this sacrifice** it is that was spoken of by the Lord: "In every place and at every time **offer me a pure sacrifice**, for I am a great king, says the Lord, and my name is wonderful among the nations."[67]

We can learn from this passage that Christians gathered on Sunday for the purpose of celebrating the Eucharist. And it is clear enough that these late 1st century Christians saw the Eucharist as a sacrifice. In fact, they even had a passage from the Old Testament that they quote here as being the proof text for this sacrifice. They paraphrase from Malachi 1:11, which, translated from the Hebrew, states:

> For from the rising of the sun to its setting my name is great among the nations, and in every place incense is offered to my name, and a pure offering;

---

[67] *Didache* 14.

for my name is great among the nations.

And so clearly the Didache views this passage from Malachi as being a prediction of the time when, in the Christian Church, the Eucharist, as a sacrifice, will be offered across the world.

This passage from the Didache is certainly the oldest extra-biblical use of this passage from Malachi as a proof text for the Eucharist as a sacrifice. But other very early Christian writers show us that this passage was the standard proof text for this doctrine.

The early Christian writer St. Justin Martyr (ca. AD 150) writes the following:

> God speaks by the mouth of Malachi, one of the twelve (minor prophets), as I said before, about **the sacrifices** at that time presented by you: ...for from the rising of the sun to the going down of the same, my name has been glorified among the gentiles, **and in every place incense is offered to my name, and a pure offering**, for my name is great among the gentiles. He speaks then of those Gentiles, namely us (Christians) who in every place **offer sacrifices to him, that is, the bread of the Eucharist and also the cup of the**

Eucharist.[68]

A bit later in that second century AD, another Christian writer, St. Irenaeus of Lyon (ca. AD 190), also knows that the passage from Malachi is the Christian proof text for the Eucharist as sacrifice. He writes:

> He took from among creation that which is bread, and gave thanks, saying, 'This is my body.' The cup likewise, which is from among the creation to which we belong, he confessed to be his blood. **He taught the new sacrifice of the new covenant, of which Malachi, one of the twelve prophets, had signified beforehand:** '...For from the rising of the sun to its setting my name is glorified among the Gentiles, and **in every place incense is offered to my name, and a pure sacrifice**; for great is my name among the Gentiles, says the Lord Almighty. By these words he makes it plain that the former people will cease to make offerings to God; but that in every place sacrifice will be offered to him, and indeed, a pure one, for his name is glorified among the Gentiles."[69]

---

[68] Justin Martyr, *Dialogue with Trypho*, 41.

[69] Irenaeus of Lyon, *Against Heresies* 4:17:5.

If all we had were the writings of St. Justin Martyr and St. Irenaeus of Lyon, we might have wondered just how early on Christians were using this passage from Malachi as a prophecy of the Eucharist as a sacrifice. From these two authors we know it is used in this way in the 2nd century AD. But when the Didache was rediscovered we suddenly found out that Christians were using that passage from Malachi in this way in the late 1st century AD as well. And so then we are left to wonder, how much earlier might the Church have been using Malachi as a prophecy for the Eucharist as a sacrifice?

The Table of the LORD

The answer is, St. Paul himself also knows the reference and he quoted from this passage while writing about the Eucharist.

The very next verse of Malachi following the passage so often quoted by the Early Church reads as follows in the Hebrew:

> But you profane it (the sacrifice) when you say that the **table of the Lord (Hebrew: šulḥan YHWH; Greek: *trapeza kuriou*)** is polluted.

Recall that St. Paul himself had called the Eucharist the "table of the Lord" in 1 Cor 10:21:

> You cannot partake of the **table of the Lord (*trapezes kuriou*)** and **the table of demons**.

The phrase "table of the Lord" occurs in the entire Bible, Old and New Testaments, in *only* two places—Malachi 1:12 and 1 Cor 10:21. That means St. Paul was indeed clearly alluding to Malachi 1:11-12 when he described the Eucharist. And therefore he believed that Malachi 1:11-12 was a prophecy of the Eucharist, one that describes the Eucharist as a sacrifice, offered from the rising of the sun until its setting.

I have demonstrated that a belief, anciently and widely held in the Church, though rejected by the early Protestant leaders because they did not believe it was found in the Bible, is indeed abundantly expressed in Sacred Scripture.

The reason the early Protestants rejected a doctrine, which they admitted was ancient and widespread, was because they did not believe the Bible taught it. The question is, why did they not see that the Bible itself did indeed teach it? What it sadly boils down to is that they did not understand that the very fact that the doctrine was ancient and widespread was strong evidence that it was believed in by the Church even in biblical times. And assuming that the doctrine, both ancient and widespread was, therefore, likely believed in by the Church in biblical times, would have allowed them to have an open enough mind to see what are, in fact, clear biblical proofs of that doctrine. An application of Intelligence Analysis would have greatly aided them toward a better interpretation of the evidence. Intelligence analysis would have instilled within them an appreciation for how a source text could seem at first glance to be silent on a matter but its author still have a strong belief that they transmitted orally to a trusted confidante.

Conclusions and Reconciliations

That the Early Church believed the Eucharist to be a sacrifice is evident, and admitted by the Protestant Reformers. That St. Paul also believed this doctrine is clear enough when he is read in light of other early Church writings such as the Didache. That millions of sincere Protestants today do not believe this, or are taught against it, is, for the Christian Church, the equivalent of a horrible intelligence failure.

And here's the even sadder fact, my dear brother or sister in Christ. You may not even be aware that the Church in which you earnestly serve our Lord came in existence at least in part over this contentious issue. Your Church may exist as a secondary split from one of the first Churches to break communion with the historical Church. The historical Church, as continued within the Catholic and Orthodox Churches, has needed and accomplished important reforms in her history. And the story of the Protestant Reformation may be that she did not accomplish some of those reforms soon enough to prevent a sad division of Christian believers. But I believe I have demonstrated in this chapter that the doctrine of the Eucharist as a Sacrifice, which we Catholics and Orthodox hold and cherish, is not something contrary to Scripture. It is taught by Scripture. And if disagreement on this doctrine was important in fueling the split, perhaps acceptance that this doctrine is not contrary to Scripture can help heal division. And I believe that approaching the Bible through the lens of Intelligence Analysis helps us to acknowledge this.

CHAPTER FIVE: IMAGE INTELLIGENCE (IMINT)

Definition of IMINT

Image intelligence is that discipline of intelligence gathering that involves photography, either captured locally or from aerial platforms, such as planes or satellites. It also potentially includes imagery related to non-visual signals, such as heat or spectra outside the range of human sight.

Who Conducts IMINT?

While some IMINT may be conducted by operatives of various intelligence agencies on a local level, the primary intelligence agency tasked with IMINT is the National Reconnaissance Office

(NRO), a division of the Department of Defense. In short, they are the agency that launches and maintains the best spy satellites our nation employs.

IMINT proper began shortly after airplanes were invented, but the combination of advances in photography and aircraft made WWII the first true theater of performance for this form of intelligence. As WWII ended, we slipped somewhat seamlessly into the Cold War with the Soviet Union, in which much of our IMINT was conducted by spy planes such as the U-2 and eventually by the SR-71. But with the launch, literally, of the Space Race, spy satellites came to supersede planes, and reduced the danger to pilots needing to fly over enemy territories, hoping to not get shot down.

Issues particular to IMINT involve mainly the challenge of interpreting what exactly an image contains. In 2003, as an NSA agent, my supervisor, myself, and other members of our office were visiting the CIA and having a collaborative session with CIA counterparts tasked with studying the same area of the world as our office (any more detail than that would be classified). They showed us an image obtained by NRO and informed us that they would be very interested in any intelligence that might corroborate what some of their analysts believed was depicted in that image. And when I say "some of their analysts," it means that other analysts disagreed. And they asked us what we thought we saw in that image. And the simple answer is, my opinion had actually been rendered null and void precisely because I had already been told what their analysts thought they saw. All I could say is, "Yes, it possibly looks like that, or maybe it's not."

Despite the ambiguity inherent in some grainy pictures, IMINT has been hugely important for the intelligence community to track the movements and activities of hostile forces and plan for military operations. But you might be wondering how a knowledge of the issues regarding IMINT could help us better understand the Bible. The answer is that IMINT today provides the faithful reader with the opportunity to understand key aspects of the Bible in ways that even the originally intended audience could not have had access to.

It's been said that in many highly successful shows on stage or screen the setting itself is one of the characters. In every Bible story you read, where characters are interacting with each other, whether it be humans with each other or God with a character of his creation, the action happened *somewhere.* And it must certainly be that the fullest grasp of the significance of the event would be attained if what we imagined the setting to be were as accurate as possible.

"Mapping" Our Mind's Eye

Growing up in Madison, Wisconsin, I recall people always saying that they were going "down to Chicago." Conversely, other times people said they were going "up to the Twin Cities." And these were natural descriptions based on the simple fact that, as you look at the map, Chicago is South of Madison (below), whereas the Twin Cities are North (above). As a result, when, as a child, I heard the Parable of the Good Samaritan, I understandably assumed that Jericho was South of Jerusalem, because, after all, the Gospel of Luke states:

> A man was going down from Jerusalem to Jericho, when he was attacked by robbers.[70]

In reality, Jericho is North-North-East from Jerusalem. The reason, however, that Luke

---

[70] Luke 10:30.

describes the man as "going down" to Jericho is that Jericho, located just 15 miles away from the Holy City, is 7200 or so feet *lower* in elevation. I saw this firsthand a few years back when my wife and I made a pilgrimage to the Holy Land. The bus ride from Jerusalem to Jericho was basically a constant steep decline, my ears popping continually from the change in elevation. And the landscape around us was desolate and arid. And I recall thinking to myself, this is where the man in the parable was attacked by robbers. When I picture that story from now on, I will always be able to imagine it happening in the place of my memories.

See it as You Read it

One way to begin applying the value of IMINT to your scriptural study is to actually go visit the places where these events took place through some sort of pilgrimage, as I did. But, as I described above, the vast majority of IMINT being conducted by the intelligence community is not done by spies on the ground, but by satellites in the sky. And you have at your disposal resources such as Google Maps, as well as limitless photos on the internet that others who have visited the sites have posted.

Like never before in history, the typical reader of the Bible can make the pages come to life with an authentic idea of what the geographical scene really looked like.

Enriching your spiritual reading in this fashion will provide you with wonderful dividends as you ground your imagination with authentic vividness.

CHAPTER SIX: LOST IN TRANSLATION

Introduction

Unless you a scholar of the original languages in which the Bible was written, you rely on a translation to access the Scriptures. In this chapter we will explore the issues that translations raise for earnest readers of the Word of God and more particularly how experiences gained from the intelligence community can help one toward a healthy and productive use of a translation in their spiritual life.

The Origins of Language

According to the book of Genesis, after the primordial flood, and after the descendents of Noah spread out over the face of the earth, there was only "one language and few words."[71] When some people decided to build a tower into the heavens, the LORD God confused their language to hinder their plan, and this was the origin of the multiple languages among humankind today.[72]

If you ascribe to a less than literal interpretation of Scripture, you could explore the available evidence from linguistic science to conclude that the wide variety of human languages spoken today have been evolving for some tens of thousands of years. And exactly how human language as we know it and use it evolved remains both a mystery and a hotly debated point. I do personally believe that human languages spoken today do all ultimately derive from a single parent. Evidence for this has been found in the observation that languages exhibit a smaller and smaller inventory of sounds the farther they are geographically from a point in West Africa.[73] Researchers have asserted that this is evidence of

---

[71] Gen 11:1.

[72] Gen 11:6-9.

[73] Atkinson, Q. D. (2011). Phonemic Diversity Supports a Serial Founder Effect Model of Language Expansion from Africa. *Science, 332*(6027), pp. 346-349. http://science.sciencemag.org/content/332/6027/346

what is called the "Serial Founder Effect," meaning that successive generations travelling away from contact with the original population lose the rich collection of sounds. While I agree this suggests a common origin of human language, I would suggest that fewer sounds in languages removed from Africa is actually evidence that the original language itself had few consonants when humanity began to spread across the face of the globe and that therefore they did not inherit a richer inventory of sounds which evolved in the parent population later.[74]

Regardless of how the diversity of human language came about, the situation today is that there are thousands of languages spoken throughout the human population. And if someone wants to grasp something written or spoken in a language they do not know, they need a translation of it into their own mode of speech.

And that's where things get interesting, both for spies and readers of the Bible.

---

[74] I presented this assertion in a video format. https://www.youtube.com/watch?v=YqSGv8CnrWs

Who Conducts Translation for the Intelligence Community?

The translation of one language into another for espionage purposes is happening actually in a variety of intelligence agencies. While not formally an intelligence agency, the State Department certainly does compile information of intelligence value and shares it with policy makers, evidenced by the contents of the diplomatic cables illegally provided to WikiLeaks by Bradley Manning (who now identifies as Chelsey Manning).[75] In the course of conducting their work, diplomats at the State Department use both their own linguistic skills and employ professional linguists to interpret live time in conversations with their counterparts and translate documents to and from the target language.

The same is true of the CIA, where a clandestine officer with the ability to speak a language will certainly be a more effective agent in terms of winning over the confidence of a potential

---

[75] For the variety of topics the diplomatic cables covered, see an early New York Times article on the subject, "Leaked Cables Offer Raw Look at US Diplomacy," by Scott Shane and Andrew W. Lehren (November 28, 2010).
https://www.nytimes.com/2010/11/29/world/29cables.html

Intel source than one who needs to bring along an interpreter.

But the intelligence agency conducting translation *par excellence* and on a scale beyond all other intelligence agencies combined is the National Security Agency, where I worked from June, 2002 until July, 2006, with the job description "Linguist." (For more detailed information on the NSA and its mission, see the chapter in this book on SIGINT.)

That I translated Arabic for the NSA is not a classified secret. Before I left the NSA, I got an unclassified resume approved by the Office of Security. It reads as follows:

> Arabic Linguist (June 2002-July 2006)
> Achieved Professional Certification as Level 3 Voice Linguist and Level 3 Graphic Linguist, passing two of the four examinations with honors.
> Through the National Security Agency, has studied Iraqi Dialect and Egyptian Dialect and used each in an operational context.
> Served at an overseas field site.
> Has worked in direct support of Operation Enduring Freedom and Operation Iraqi Freedom.
> Holding Clearance Level of TOP SECRET (TS)/Sensitive Compartmented Information (SCI)/Special intelligence(SI)/TALENT-KEYHOLE (TK) and has had an Agency Special Background

Investigation (SBI) and polygraph.

The fact that I additionally served in Iraq, while not included in this resume, is an unclassified fact because references to it appear in my book *Top Secrets: Lessons for Success from the World of Espionage*, which the NSA approved for publication, as well as by the fact that the NSA itself later issued me the Global War on Terrorism Civilian Service Medal, the criteria of which were met while serving there.

Translation at the NSA

Obviously what I actually translated was Top Secret and remains so to this day. But, bringing this back to the issue of translation and the Bible, for four years my full time job was translating materials from Arabic into English for the purpose of someone else then taking the product of my work and turning it into a report that would be disseminated to governmental policy makers, including the White House.

No matter how good the translator is, at the NSA the translation is always double checked by another senior linguist in a process called Quality Control (QC). This ensures accuracy of the details that will then be going into intelligence reports. Sometimes the reporters actually writing the reports would come back to the linguists and ask whether there might be some nuance in a specific part of the message that could justify an inference the reporter might want to include. And the linguists, both original translator and QCer would discuss the matter in collaboration with the reporter. It was an intellectually stimulating environment in which I had the privilege to work alongside women and men employing our talents in defense of our great nation.

As a result of working in that setting, and having my undergraduate degree in Greek and Latin and my PhD in Biblical Hebrew, I can certainly call myself an expert in the subject of translation as it relates to the Bible. I will now explore with you a history of biblical translation and share with you practical advice for how to select and use a translation for your own spiritual nourishment.

The Hebrew Bible Before Translations

The Hebrew Bible began coming into its current form after the Jewish people returned from exile in Babylon. It is divided into three major sections, the Law (*Torah*) the Prophets (*Nevi'im*) and the Writings (*Ketuvim*). Although the Jews would not formally crystallize their canon of Scripture in this arrangement until after the destruction of the 2nd Temple (AD 69), this arrangement of their books was already in place long before. In Luke 24:44, Jesus says:

> Everything which was written about me in the Law of Moses and the Prophets and the Psalms must be fulfilled.

Since the book of Psalms is the first book in that section later known as "Writings," this is a clear reference to that tripartite arrangement of Hebrew Scriptures decades before it was formalized.

The Jews had successfully survived the exile by learning how to thrive in Diaspora and maintain their religious and cultural identity. Jeremiah himself had pointed the way when he directed those in exile:

> Seek the wholeness of the city where I have sent you into exile, and pray to the LORD on its behalf; for in its wholeness you will have wholeness.[76]

And so the Jews in Babylon multiplied there and were able to return to their land a vigorous people capable of rebuilding their nation. But there were plenty of Jews who stayed in Babylon and continued to thrive. And after the Greeks under Alexander took control of the entire eastern Mediterranean and then the Persian Empire, Jews formed communities in places such as Alexandria. Following the advice of Jeremiah, they became contributors to the welfare of the place they lived, while maintaining their religious and cultural identity.

Time to Translate

In the course of time, there were Jews in places such as Egypt who did not have a command of Hebrew sufficient to understand their own sacred Scriptures. Sometime in the mid 200's BC, that translation of Jewish Scripture into Greek known as the Septuagint (LXX) was undertaken.

---

[76] Jer 29:7.

According to the 2nd century BC *Letter of Aristeas*, this translation was commissioned by Pharaoh Ptolemy II Philadelphus (285–246 BC) so that the writings of the Jews could be accessible to Greek scholars in his realm. According to this letter, the Pharaoh secured 72 translators, six from each of the 12 Tribes of Israel. They each worked independently and each worked for exactly 72 days and each produced the exact same translation.[77]

Now, this is obviously a fanciful account designed to make people esteem this Greek translation as having an authority on par with the Hebrew original. But this translation was indeed widely used and venerated. Even though the authors of the New Testament, with the exception of St. Luke, seem to have been native speakers of Aramaic and versed in Hebrew, they directly quote the Septuagint translation at least half of the time.

In fact, the New Testament not only contains abundant direct quotes from the Septuagint version, it contains at least one quote from the Old Testament that appears only in the Septuagint and not in the Hebrew Version at all. When Hebrews 1:6 quotes from the Book of Jeremiah 31:43, we read:

---

[77] *Letter of Aristeas*, 301-311.

And let all the angels of God worship him.

But this particular line does not occur in the Hebrew version, only in the Septuagint.

And so, even in ancient times, believers came to rely on translations. In the case of the Septuagint, the translation itself was so revered that there are cases where the translation contains the key wording upon which a doctrinal point is made.

As my primary advice to you, I would just have you approach the Bible always fully aware that, unless you are reading it in the original languages, you are indeed reading it through the filter of fallible humans who have, with varying degrees of success or even intention, tried to convert the actual Bible into an English language version you can understand. And the implication of this could indeed be that you both look at multiple translations as you study the Bible but also that you would actively seek out knowledge of potential biases that a translation may have introduced.

Translation versus Interpretation

A well-known example of an *intentional* bias introduced into a translation is found in John 1:1

of the *New World Translation*, produced by the Jehovah's Witnesses. First, the original Greek with a literal translation:

> *En arche en ho logos, kai ho logos en pros ton theon,* **kai theos en ho logos**
> In the beginning was the Word. And the Word was with God. **And God was the Word**.

Because Jehovah's Witnesses do not hold the Trinitarian belief in the divinity of Jesus, they add a word to their translation that is not in the Greek at all.

> ***New World Translation***
> In the beginning was the Word. And the Word was with God. And the Word ***was a god*** (emphasis my own).

So what other actual truths might be either obscured or even hidden by intentional biased translations? To explore this issue more fully, I will present for you yet another case where the New Testament message completely relies on a translation—the Greek LXX—and then continue into a comparison of English translations on a contentious point of doctrine.

The Virgin Birth of Jesus

In Matthew 1:23, the fact that Mary was pregnant without having had sexual relations is described as fulfilling a prophecy:

> Behold, a **virgin** shall conceive and bear a son, and his name shall be called Emmanuel (which means, God with us).

The Greek word for 'virgin' here is *parthenos*. But the Hebrew original of this passage from Isaiah 7:14 does not use the Hebrew word for virgin (which would be *betulah*), but rather the word which generically means 'young woman', *'almah*. If you go read the whole passage in Isaiah 7:10-17, the statement that an "*'almah* shall conceive and bear a son" is not a future prediction, nor is it even a miracle. Rather, the context of the passage in Isaiah itself is about King Ahaz being given a sign for how long a period of time it will take until his enemies would be thwarted, namely, the time period it would take for a young woman to A) conceive and bear a son and B) for the child to grow up enough to eat solid food and know what tastes he likes and does not. In other words, in roughly just two to three years, King Ahaz will not need to worry about those enemies any more.

But we cannot deny that the Evangelist St. Matthew quotes from the Greek version precisely because the use of the word *parthenos* predicts a miracle he tells us is fulfilled in the conception of Jesus. This fact shows us once again how very important and authoritative the Greek translation, the LXX, was to the early Church. It seems that the Jewish translators had already come to believe that this passage from Isaiah, even if it did in its original context refer to a short term prediction about the enemies of King Ahaz, also contained a long term prophecy about the coming Messiah. And they made their translation unambiguously describe a future miracle.

I would assert that even without this passage from the Prophet Isaiah, the Virgin Birth of Jesus could have occurred as a miracle without fulfilling any scriptural promise. The fact that translators had included a messianic interpretation into their translation could have been a happy coincidence or even Divine Providence, but it has no bearing whatsoever on the doctrine of the Virgin Birth of Jesus, which is clearly taught in the Gospels of Matthew and Luke.

Let's stay on this general topic and now explore how English translations may include bias on the ancient Church teaching that St. Mary not only was a virgin when she gave birth to Jesus, but remained so her entire life.

The Ever-Virginity of Mary

The early Church scholar (and the man who produced the Church's official translation of the Bible into Latin) St. Jerome, defending the teaching that St. Mary was a virgin her entire life, wrote that this teaching was held and taught by:

> "Ignatius, Polycarp, Irenaeus, Justin Martyr, and many other apostolic and eloquent men..."[78]

If what St. Jerome writes is true, it would mean that the belief that St. Mary was a virgin her whole life was a part of Church teaching from the very beginning. Sts. Ignatius, Polycarp, Irenaeus, and Justin Martyr lived and wrote in the first two centuries of Christian history. St. Jerome certainly did have access to writing from these men which are now lost to us. What we do have left from the writings of those early saints does not contain an explicit formulation of the teaching of Mary's ever-

---

[78] St. Jerome, *Against Helvidius* 19.

virginity. But St. Jerome could not have made such a claim if it were not verifiable.

I believe there is an extant explicit reference to St. Mary as ever-Virgin dating from around the end of the 1st century AD. The Syriac Odes of Solomon are an early Christian collection of hymns, which contain the following remarkable description of the Virgin Birth:

> The Spirit opened the womb of **the Virgin** and she received conception and brought forth; and **the Virgin** became a Mother with many mercies; And she was in labor and brought forth a Son, without feeling pain.[79]

The fact that the original Syriac consistently calls her "the Virgin" (*betulta*) I find quite significant. The Odist is not just telling us that "a Virgin" gave birth, as if the virginal and miraculous birth were itself the focus and the woman involved a mere biological necessity. Rather, by calling her "*the* Virgin," the Odist is showing a veneration of her and also giving her a title that would be quite impossible if the writer believed that St. Mary later went on to have other

---

[79] *Odes of Solomon* 19.6-7.

biological children.

Nevertheless, the question of exactly how early on Christians were believing in the Ever-Virginity of Mary is meaningless to those who only find their religious authority in the Bible. An exploration of the verses in the New Testament that speak to this question—and how various English translation either admit or obscure their potential role in this argument—will now be our current study.

The Brothers of Jesus

The primary reason for believing that St. Mary had other children after she gave birth to Jesus are references to the "Brothers of the Lord." A representative reference is the following:

> [People said], Is not this the carpenter's son? Is not his mother called Mary? And are not his brothers James and Joseph and Simon and Judas? And are not all his sisters with us?[80]

It should be noted that those who believe in the Virgin Birth but yet also use this verse as evidence

---

[80] Matthew 13:55-56. See also Mark 3:31-32; Mark 6:3; 1 Corinthians 9:5; Galatians 1:19.

that Jesus had biological siblings apparently ignore the line "Is not this the carpenter's son?" If you believe the people speaking here were wrong about him actually being "the carpenter's son," then you cannot place credence on their words regarding his so-called brothers!

Early proponents of the belief that Mary had no further children after Jesus describe these so-called "Brothers (and Sisters) of the Lord" as either his half-siblings (from an earlier marriage of Joseph) or as cousins. It is certainly true that Aramaic, the language Jesus and his disciples (and family) spoke, as well as Hebrew, did not have a separate word for half-sibling or cousin. For example, in Genesis 13:8, Abram says to his nephew Lot:

> Let there not be any strife between you and me ... because we are brothers (*'ḥym*).

Later, Abram rescues Lot from a group of kings and we read:

> ...and he also brought back his brother (*'ḥyw*) Lot...[81]

---

[81] Genesis 14:16.

Nevertheless, the fact that references to "Brothers of Jesus" *could* mean cousins does not mean they *probably* are. If we were studying Scripture apart from Church Traditions, we would likely be safe to assume that the most direct interpretation of the Bible is that references to the "Brothers of Jesus" do mean that St. Mary did have other children, unless there were other points of evidence in the New Testament that tilted the scales a different direction.

Fragments from a late 1st/early 2nd century disciple of the Apostle St. John, a man named Papias include how Papias states that the brothers of Jesus are actually the children of a sister of Jesus' mother, who was also named Mary.[82] Let's see whether the New Testament itself would support this assertion.

How Many Jameses?

We read in Matthew 27:56 that, watching the crucifixion from afar, were:

> ...Mary Magdalene and Mary, the mother of James and Joseph...

---

[82] *Fragments of Papias* 10.

The parallel passage in Mark describes them as:

>...Mary Magdalene and Mary the mother of James the younger and of Joses...[83]

It is clear that describing this St. James as "the younger" is a way to distinguish him from one who is somehow older/greater. And the only candidate for such a James would be St. James the son of Zebedee, one of the actual 12 Disciples, which James the younger was not. But this would further mean that there are not several men known as James running around this circle of personalities. In essence, there is James, the son of Zebedee and there is the other James, the one who is the son of the other Mary.[84]

St. Mary had a Sister Named ... Mary?

The argument would be clinched if the New Testament actually describes St. Mary, the mother of Jesus as having a sister/kinswoman also named

---

[83] Mark 15:40.

[84] Matthew 28:1.

Mary. And the Bible does just that. Note the following:

> Standing by the cross of Jesus were his mother, and his mother's sister, Mary the wife of Clopas, and Mary Magdalene.[85]

How many women were standing there? If you work only from this English translation and assume that things like commas (which did not exist in New Testament times) are how you divide up a list, you might decide this is a list of four women:

1) His mother
2) His mother's sister
3) Mary the wife of Clopas
4) Mary Magdalene

But there weren't commas in ancient times. The way you divide up a list of people is ordinarily to use the word *and* (*kai*). For instance, in Matthew 10:2-4, the 12 Disciples of Jesus are named, and every single one of them is separated from the others with the word *and* (*kai*):

---

[85] John 19:25.

These are the names of the 12 Disciples: First
Simon, the one called Peter AND Andrew his
brother AND James the son of Zebedee AND his
brother John AND (etc)..."

The original Greek of the list of women standing at the cross reads as follows:

His mother AND (*kai*) his mother's sister, Mary the wife of Clopas, AND (*kai*) Mary Magdalene.

The most natural interpretation of this would be that there are actually only three women there. And his mother's sister *is* Mary, the wife of Clopas.

But look for a moment at the NIV translation of the verse in question:

Near the cross of Jesus stood his mother, his mother's sister, Mary the wife of Clopas, and Mary Magdalene.

Notice, they actually *removed* the first "and" (which is found in the Greek original) in order to make their translation seem even more strongly to be describing a list of four women! Don't think that this was done with no thought to the fact that this verse is important to Catholic/Orthodox teaching. Sadly, this is yet another example of how earnest and innocent readers of the Bible end up reading more than just the Word of God, they are reading a human interpretation, which in this case is actually designed to teach (and simultaneously to refute) a specific belief.

Understanding the Word "Until"

As long as we're on this general topic, there is another verse of the New Testament where the particular translation you are reading may be trying to teach you that Mary had other children, even if the verse of the Bible in question is ambiguous on the point.

In Matthew 1:25, we read, in the Revised Standard Version (RSV) that St. Joseph took St. Mary as his wife:

but knew her not until she had borne a son.

I am a native speaker of English. You probably are as well. And our native speaker instinct is that the word "until" strongly implies that while a thing did not happen prior to a certain point, it *did* happen afterwards.

In other words, even if, as the RSV states, St. Joseph did not have sexual relations with St. Mary "until" she gave birth to Jesus, he is understood, by native speakers of English, to have done so afterwards.

But is that what the Greek original actually says? Because, remember, all we have studied in terms of the implications of intelligence analysis upon Biblical Study tell us that the only important matter is what the Greek original actually says and means to a native speaker of Greek. Whatever multiple translations might say and imply is meaningless.

The Greek word here translated as "until" is *heos*. Remember that in the intelligence community, a report that is sent to policy makers should not—must not—contain even so much as an implication unless the original message that led up to the report fully justifies it. In other words, translating *heos* as "until" is either fine or horrible, depending on whether the word really does mean "until." If, instead, the word actually just means "prior to" (with no implication whatsoever about what happened afterwards), then the translation "until" would be not just inaccurate, but actually misleading. Such an English translation would teach something that the Greek original itself did not teach.

To get to the bottom of this, we need to look at other uses of the Greek word *heos* and see whether or not a translation of "until" is better than "prior to."

To repeat, the English word "until" is a great word when we really do mean to state that something did not happen until after something else happened (but that something else did indeed happen after that first thing).

Here are English examples highlighting the difference:

> 1) Mary did not meet Joseph until she met James.
> 2) Mary did not meet Joseph prior to meeting James.

Number 1 is understood by native speakers of English to imply that Mary did indeed meet Joseph, but only after she had met James. Number 1 might as well be worded:

> 1) Mary did not meet Joseph until after she had met James.

But Number 2 is ambiguous. In Number 2, it is possible that Mary never met Joseph at all. While it is also possible that she did, Number 2 does not state she *necessarily* did.

But here it is important to point out that the two clauses of Matthew 1:25 contains different subjects and objects. In other words, the better comparison would be the following formulation:

1a) Joseph did not meet Mary until Mary visited the Grand Canyon.

Here we are left confused. Did they meet at all? We can make it unambiguous by added the word "after":

1b) Joseph did not meet Mary until after Mary visited the Grand Canyon.

In Number 1b we do believe they met. In Number 1a, we may think so, but we aren't sure. Now look at this:

2a) Joseph did not meet Mary prior to Mary visiting the Grand Canyon.

In Number 2a we can at least imagine a context in which Joseph wanted to meet Mary, but never did, since, after all, she visited the Grand Canyon:

Joseph very much wanted to meet Mary. But he knew that she was going on that trip to visit the Grand Canyon and then would be moving to Europe, never to return again. Joseph did not meet

Mary prior to Mary visiting the Grand Canyon. And that's why they never met at all.

Whether or not the Greek word *heos* actually means "until" or "prior to" is crucial to the question of whether the New Testament allows or refutes the Catholic/Orthodox teaching of Mary being Ever-Virgin. And also, context will be everything.

Let's do what any good intelligence analyst would do—examine the available data. But before we look at parallel cases, it should be noted that if we were to take Matthew 1:25 ***very*** literally and understand *heos* as implying that the second action did indeed happen after the first, then the verse would be stating that St. Joseph had sexual relations with St. Mary *immediately* after she gave birth, which would be both absurd and also a violation of Mosaic Law.[86] This issue was spotted by St. Jerome himself.[87] And the fact is, there does not live today any scholar of biblical languages who can claim to know New Testament Greek better than St. Jerome, who learned and studied it at a time when it was still a spoken language.

---

[86] Leviticus 12:2-4; Luke 2:22.

[87] St. Jerome, *Against Helvidius* 10.

The fact is, the word *heos* does not always mean "until" in Greek. It also certainly does not always imply that the action described afterwards necessarily took place. Note the following counter-example:

> And Michal the daughter of Saul had no child until (*heos*) the day of her death.[88]

It goes without saying that she did not have a child on or after the day of her death! (She did not die in childbirth.)

Matthew 1:25 is ambiguous, but it certainly does not serve as an obvious proof text for Mary and Joseph having sexual relations. If it were, why would scholars so much closer in time and better versed than we are today in New Testament Greek not have seen it that way? Indeed, even the early Protestant Reformers did not understand Matthew 1:25 as arguing against the Ever-Virginity of St. Mary.

Martin Luther:

---

[88] 2 Samuel 6:23.

When Matthew says that Joseph did not know Mary carnally until she had brought forth her son, it does not follow that he knew her subsequently; on the contrary, it means that he never did know her.[89]

Note also that the Latin text of the 1537 AD Smalcald Articles (a statement of Lutheran belief), which was written by Martin Luther himself, states that Jesus was born from:

Mary, pure, holy, **ever-virgin**
*ex Maria, pura, sancta, **sempervirgine***[90]

Caveat Lector: Let the Reader Beware

In the final analysis, all I have been getting at is to stress that every translation is an interpretation that invariably includes the opinion of the translator. If the translator happens to believe what the biblical writer intended when he wrote a particular book, then the translation should be an accurate window into the Bible itself. But to the

---

[89] Martin Luther, "That Jesus Christ was Born a Jew," in Luther's Works 45:211-212.

[90] Martin Luther, Smalcald Articles 1.4, 1537.

extent that a modern translator includes even so much as a nuance that the original writer would not have agreed with, then the so-called translation is anything but. It pushes the actual Bible away from the eager eyes of the faithful.

If this is all true, then how can we even claim to know and read the Bible at all? Here's where I will answer that ultimate question by bringing us back to the world of intelligence analysis. Unless you are a linguist, reading the original text, and understanding it with the full collective knowledge of the community that produced it and received it, you are not actually reading the Bible at all.

Christians would do well to adopt the attitude Islam has toward the idea of "translating" Scripture. In Islam, a rendering of the Arabic language Qur'an into another language is called an "interpretation (*tafsir*)," not a "translation (*tarjama*)." Indicative of this idea, the British convert to Islam Marmaduke Pickthall (1875-1936) titled his "translation" *The Meaning of the Glorious Koran*, not "The Koran."

It may seem a little and insignificant change, but Bible translations should openly state what they are—translations. Instead, the prevailing tendency with at least English language translations is to refer to them all as "versions," for example, the Revised Standard Version (RSV) or the New International Version (NIV). Calling something a "version" hides the reality that it is a translation project, normally of multiple people who have human flaws, opinions, and agendas.

Understanding the Bible Through Tradition

The closest we can come to actually reading the Bible is to allow the author herself to read it to us and explain to us what it means. Note that when St. Philip was led by the Spirit to his encounter with the Ethiopian eunuch, he heard the man reading from the book of Isaiah and he asked him:

Do you understand what you are reading?[91]

The eunuch's response should be the response of all of us when it comes to understanding the Bible:

How can I unless someone guides me?[92]

---

[91] Acts 8:30.

[92] Acts 8:31.

St. Philip was able to explain what the eunuch was reading because he had the mind of the Church. As intelligence analysis would teach us, the actual truth of what an utterance originally meant could only be fully known and understood by pulling together a great cloud of witnesses who were both contemporaries of the biblical authors and also the immediate descendents of the Apostles themselves. In other words, for any verse where we might wonder what it actually means, our first question should be, "What did the Ancient Church, so much closer to the *author*, believe this meant?"

The Bible, as a linguistic artifact, is a fascinating thing to study. And we are the inheritors of thousands of years of attempts to make it known to us through translations into the languages of those who did not know the original. But the Bible, understood only through a human translation, simply cannot carry the weight that many Christians would place upon it. How then did God intend us to know the truth which would set us free?

The manifold wisdom of God is made known to us "through the Church."[93] The Church, the

---

[93] Ephesians 3:10.

household of God, is the "Pillar and Bulwark of the Truth."[94]

She wrote the New Testament. She hand-copied it and passed it down for generations and generations. What she believes it means is the Gospel Truth.

---

[94] 1 Timothy 3:15.

CHAPTER SEVEN: SECRET CODES (DECIPHERMENT) IN THE BIBLE

Secret Codes in the Bible

People revere the Bible and believe it contains Divine Wisdom. It is not surprising, therefore, that some people would further believe that the Bible contains secret information for those who can crack its code. In this chapter we will explore together legitimate cases of secret codes in the Bible, but also learn why many other claims to have found hidden information in Scripture are fraudulent.

I've always been fascinated by mysteries. And even before I went to the NSA, I had published my proposed solution to an ancient linguistic puzzle. The holy book of Islam, the Qur'an, contains a series of seemingly random letters that begin several of the chapters. I published an article in 1996 in which I argued that the letters were not really random at all, but were ordered lists of the abbreviated names of people consulted as sources for the wording of these chapters.[95]

But when I came to the NSA, I had the opportunity to take a week-long course in cryptographic methods. It taught me all the techniques of how to both encrypt and decrypt a message that had been used up to the period of World War II, when early computers took over the task. And I learned how to spot and exploit patterns that could unlock the key to a secret message.

Cracking a "Secret" Code on the Job!

While still at the NSA, I had the opportunity to put my new talents to the test. In a December while I was there, a message had been sent to some government agency. It was a seemingly random series of numbers, apparently a code of some kind. The NSA sent it out to all employees

---

[95] "A New Investigation into the 'Mystery Letters' of the Qur'an," by Keith Massey, in *Arabica, Vol. 43 No. 3*. (1996), pp. 497–501.

with a request that people try to decipher it. I looked at it and immediately spotted that several of the "words" started with the same two numbers.

I followed the hypothesis that this was a message in the Arabic language. The word in Arabic for "the" is *al-*. And it's prefixed to the word it modifies. So I wrote out AL everywhere I saw that pattern, including other places those numbers appeared. I spotted that there was a word in the message that was only three letters long, but it started with "AL." I assumed this was the common Arabic preposition "to" (transliterated as ALI). From there other words opened up. Within minutes I had deciphered the message. It stated that nuclear bombs would soon be going off in Washington, New York, and Chicago.

My heart was racing as I rushed to the office that had sent out this cryptographic challenge. As I was approaching the door, a woman I had worked with previously was also arriving there. I knew her to be a skilled cryptographer. I blurted out half the message. She shouted out the rest. We burst through the door and presented our findings jointly to the requesting office.

We would later learn that the "code" in question was a known "aspirational message," meaning, it was something that Jihadists had been posting widely on open sources, with high hopes but no credibility (obviously, since it did not happen). The particular form that we had "deciphered" had defaulted the Arabic letters to numbers during a copy and paste function. In other words, this message had been accidentally, and unintentionally, turned into a cryptographic puzzle.

Even so, the office that issued the challenge was grateful that analysts at the NSA had been able to decipher the puzzle and at least relieve the intelligence community that we had not missed some important secret message. The other analyst and I were jointly given a cash reward for our efforts that made Christmas that year a lot more merry.

It is important to point out that this message was only able to be deciphered because the letters had been turned into numbers consistently and with no erroneous values introduced. If even a portion of the numbers had been randomly changed, the original message would have been unrecoverable. And that is ultimately why finding truly secret messages encoded in large portions of the Bible is impossible. As we learned earlier, the handwritten copies of the Bible over the centuries randomly introduced multiple errors which would completely throw off any ability to recover a "secret code," even if one had been inserted in the text.

Other Decipherments

Since I have left the NSA, I have published proposed decipherments of a number of ancient mysteries. For instance, I published a proposed decipherment of the enigmatic Ezerovo Ring, one of the few examples of Dacian writing.[96] I also released a mathematical interpretation of the oldest example of human writing ever discovered, the Tartaria Tablets.[97]

Another effort, and by far the most notable, is my proposed decipherment of the 250 year old mystery known as the Shugborough Inscription. My solution to this enigma was reported in the *Birmingham Post* and I was interviewed by the

---

[96] "Further Evidence for an 'Italic' Substratum in Romanian," by Keith Massey in *Philologie im Netz* 43/2008, pp. 11-16.

http://web.fu-berlin.de/phin/phin43/p43t2.htm

[97] To study my proposals, visit my website:

http://aplaceofbrightness.blogspot.com/

BBC's *World Update* concerning my research.[98]

Decipherments in the Bible Itself

Simply put, the process of encryption and decipherment is putting information into a form that it hidden, unintelligible—to conceal it from others, and then extracting that information again so someone you want to know about it can understand it. The earliest example in the Bible of someone "deciphering" a secret message is the Patriarch Joseph, who, we learn in the book of Genesis, had the power to interpret dreams. Interestingly, long before Joseph successfully interpreted (deciphered) dreams in Egypt, he showed the ability to have a predictive dream. We read in Genesis 37: 5-7:

> And Joseph dreamt a dream and he declared it to his brothers. And it made them hate him even

---

[98] "200-Year-Old Mystery of Shugborough Code 'Solved'," by Mike Lockley. *Birmingham Post*, December 21, 2014.

http://www.birminghampost.co.uk/news/regional-affairs/200-year-old-mystery-shugborough-code-solved-8319385/

BBC World Update interview with Dan Damon on 12/24/2014.

more. And he said to them, "Listen to this dream that I have dreamt. Behold, we were binding sheaves in the field and my sheaf arose and stood up and behold, your sheaves gathered around it and bowed down to my sheaf."

This is, of course, exactly what would come to pass when the brothers much later come to Egypt seeking grain during a famine.[99] The brothers' negative reaction upon hearing this dream suggests that this is not the first time Joseph has either had a predictive dream or successfully interpreted that of another. In Genesis 37:8 they replied:

> Are you really going to rule over us? Or are you really going to have dominion over us?" And so they hated him all the more because of his dreams and his words.

It should be noted, that Joseph's brothers here successfully interpret the dream. They know that the sheaves of each stand for each man and that therefore a sheaf bowing down means that the person will bow down. This already sets the stage for the fact that, in the Book of Genesis, dream

---

[99] Gen 42:6.

interpretation is not rocket science. The dreams presented in this account are fairly transparent, and decipherment of them certainly does not require a supercomputer.

Joseph had yet another similar dream and this one even manages to anger his father. We read in Genesis 37:9-11:

> And he dreamed yet another dream and he told it to his brothers. And he said, "Behold, I have dreamt another dream and behold, the sun, the moon, and eleven stars bowed down to me." And when he told it to his father and to his brothers, his father rebuked him and said to him, "What is this dream which you have dreamt? Will I and your mother and your brothers come and bow down to the ground to you?" And his brothers were jealous of him, but his father kept the matter in his heart.

It is curious that Jacob understands the dream to imply that Joseph's mother Rachel will, along with him and the brothers, bow down to her son, since she is reported to have already died during the birth of Benjamin.[100] He cannot mean Rachel's sister Leah as a sort of surrogate mother following Rachel's death, since Leah also seems to have died

---

[100] Genesis 35:17-19.

before Jacob himself journeyed to Egypt.[101] The only reasonable explanation is that sometimes predictive dreams can be mostly, but not completely, true.

It is Joseph's ability to interpret (again, decipher) dreams that will really help him find his fortune in life. His brothers sell him into slavery in Egypt, telling Jacob that he was killed by wild animals.[102] He is bought by Potiphar, an Egyptian official and is then thrown in prison after turning down the sexual advances of Potiphar's wife.[103] While in prison, two fellow inmates one day share with Joseph the dreams that they have had, and Joseph tells them what the dreams mean and predict for their futures.

Pharaoh's former chief butler tells his dream first:

> In my dream there was a vine in front of me, and on the vine there were three branches. As soon as it sprouted, its blossoms came forth, and the clusters became grapes. Pharaoh's cup was in my hand and I took the grapes and pressed them into Pharaoh's

---

[101] Gen 49:31.

[102] Gen 37:12-36.

[103] Genesis 39:1-23.

cup, and I put the cup in Pharaoh's hand."[104]

Joseph had previously told the two fellow inmates that "interpretations belong to God."[105] Even so, a dream in which you are once again doing that which you used to do can only mean that you will do that thing again, I mean, if dreams are reliably predictive of the future. So Joseph interprets it accordingly:

> This is its interpretation. The three branches are three days. Within three days Pharaoh will lift up your head and reinstall you in your position. And you will put Pharaoh's cup in his hand as before, when you were his butler.[106]

We must grant that viewing the branches as days is not, in fact, a no-brainer, and so Joseph does have some divine spark as he performs this decipherment. He asks the butler to remember him and speak favorably of him if he ever has occasion, since he is an innocent man.[107]

---

[104] Gen 40:9-11.

[105] Gen 40:8.

[106] Gen 40:12-13.

[107] Gen 40:14-15.

Pharaoh's chief baker goes next:

> I also in my dream, there were three baskets on my head. And in the top basket there were all kinds of the foods for Pharaoh, but birds were eating it from the basket on my head.[108]

Carrion birds eating road kill is a well enough known concept that the dream is by no means good news. Joseph manages to insert some dark humor into his response and makes a play on words when he told the butler that Pharaoh would "lift his head":

> This is its interpretation. The three baskets are three days. Within three days Pharaoh will lift up your head—from upon you! And he will hang you on a tree and the birds will eat the flesh from you.[109]

All these things came to pass and in the course of time Pharaoh himself had disturbing dreams he wanted interpreted:

---

[108] Gen 40:16-17.

[109] Gen 40:18-19.

After two years Pharaoh dreamed that he was standing next to the Nile. And behold, there came out of the Nile seven cows, sleek and fat. And they fed upon the reeds. And behold seven other cows came up after them out of the Nile, thin and gaunt, and stood next to the other cows on the banks of the Nile. And the thin and gaunt cows ate the seven sleek and fat cows. And Pharaoh woke up. And he fell asleep and dreamed a second time. And behold, there were seven ears of grain, plump and good, which were growing on one stalk. And behold seven ears sprouted after them, thin and blighted by the east wind. And the thin ears swallowed the seven plumb and good ears. And Pharaoh awoke and behold, it was a dream.[110]

Joseph successfully interpreted this dream into a prediction of seven years of plenty, followed by seven years of famine. And Pharaoh wisely realized that the perfect person to be put in charge of a grand project of saving surplus against the years of want would be the very man who predicted all this—Joseph himself. Joseph became a great man, and all of it came about because of his ability to interpret/decipher, if you will, encoded messages sent to the world from God in the form of dreams. Again, the overall point here is that the dream is a

---

[110] Gen 41:1-7.

message that God *wanted* to be deciphered. It is not impossibly obscure.

Daniel and the "Writing on the Wall"

The biblical case of a true linguistic decipherment *par excellence* is found in the story of how Daniel deciphers the mysterious message written on a wall in the reign of King Belshazzar, son of King Nebuchadnezzar (6th century BC).[111] While the king was at a feast and wining and dining a thousand guests, he ordered that gold and silver vessels taken out of the Temple in Jerusalem be used as glasses by himself and his guests. Suddenly the fingers of a man's hand appeared and wrote on the plaster of the wall of the king's palace. The king saw this and asked his wise men and astrologers to interpret the message. When they could not, eventually Daniel, who had served Nebuchadnezzar, was brought in. The "secret" message and Daniel's interpretation are as follows:

---

[111] Even though the book of Daniel is set during the period of the Babylonian Exile, scholars have uncovered a number of linguistic and contextual reasons why the book likely was written much later than that. See *Daniel: A Commentary* by Carol A. Newsom, pp. 6-11 (2014: Westminster John Know Press).

MENE MENE TEQEL and *PARSIN*[112]

What is interesting here is that the "interpretation" here does seem to rely not on Daniel's inspiration, but on his linguistic knowledge, since he interprets these words as not uncommon Semitic words. I will show you the Aramaic word in his interpretation which is clearly playing off the root of the deciphered message. He proclaims:

> *MENE*, God has numbered (*mena*) the days of your kingdom and brought it to an end.
> *TEQEL*, you have been weighed (*teqilta*) in the balances and found wanting.
> *PERES*, your kingdom is divided (*perisat*) and given to the Medes and Persians (*paras*).[113]

In exchange for this successful interpretation (despite how negatively it seemed to portend Belshazzar's future), Daniel was made third ruler in the kingdom. But that very night Belshazzar was killed and Darius the Mede took over in his place.

---

[112] Daniel 5:25.

[113] Daniel 5:26-28.

The Bible is Not a Mystery

Apart from such overt cases in which someone interprets something previously unknown, the Bible is not primarily obscure and an enigma to be deciphered. As I mentioned earlier, any actual elaborate secret code placed in the letters of the Bible would have long ago been made irretrievable by even such minor textual corruptions as we know occurred during the handwritten transmission of biblical manuscripts. As I have stressed in this book, intelligence analysis teaches us that the Bible, like any sample of language, was readily intelligible to native speakers among its original audience. It may be, as in the case of one of St. Paul's Epistles, that the original audience that would understand all of it was a small group of people, with the possibility that even in his lifetime people did not completely understand the significance of every reference. But the Bible was not written to be a secret code.

Possible Secret Messages in Ancient Literatures

There are a few intriguing examples of possible hidden messages in ancient literatures. For instance, there is the intriguing possibility that the Roman poet Publius Vergilius Maro (Vergil) has hidden his signature in the first four lines of his magnum opus, the Aeneid:[114]

Arma uirumque cano, Troiae qui primus ab oriS
Italiam fato profugus Lauiniaque ueniT
Litora – multum ille et terris iactatus et altO
Vi superum, saeuae memorem Iunonis ob iraM

If you read the first and last letters of these four lines right, left, right and again left, they produce:

A STILO MV

This is translated as:

From the pen of M(aro) V(ergilius)

Is this a pure coincidence? There is also the possibility that the author of the biblical book of Esther has similarly hidden a secret message in the text. While the book does not overtly mention God at all, it may be that the Divine Name is still found

---

[114] Following Aratus' plow : Vergil's signature in the "Aeneid, by Christiano Castelletti in *Museum Helveticum* Vol. 69, No. 1 (June 2012), pp. 83-95.

encoded in the book in the following fashion:

Esther 5:4
Let the king and Haman come today
*Ybw' **H**mlk **W**hmn **H**ywm*

The first letters of these four Hebrew words are the name of God *YHWH*.[115] Coincidence? Personally, I think it is probably just that, a coincidence.

In the final analysis, uncovering secret codes hidden in the Bible would require the exact text as originally written to have been perfectly passed down, which, as we learned earlier in the book, did not quite take place. Apart from cases such as I have described above, in which biblical characters did have to solve riddles and interpret dreams, the Bible itself is not a repository of secret knowledge. Quite the contrary, it was written to instruct all who read it, not just a few who might crack its code.

---

[115] Similar acrostics are also found in Esther 1:20, 5:13, and 7:7.

CHAPTER EIGHT: ASSESSING THE EYEWITNESSES OF THE RESURRECTION

Did Jesus Really Rise from the Dead? A Former Spy Evaluates the Reliability of the Claim

Before I even start, in the interest of full disclosure and transparency, I remind you that I am a priest of the Eastern Orthodox Church. I believe in the Resurrection of Jesus.

But I am also a former spy. For four years after 9/11 I worked as an Arabic linguist at the Top Secret National Security Agency. I was awarded the Global War on Terrorism Civilian Service Medal for service in Iraq in 2004 while working there.

I will examine the claim the Apostles made that

Jesus rose from the dead using the same criteria that the intelligence community uses for assessing the reliability of human intelligence sources. And it is important to keep in mind that how reliable and accurate a claim is has nothing to do with whether it is ultimately true.

I will tell you right now that I will not be concluding that an intelligence assessment of the available information means you should believe that the Resurrection of Jesus is probably, or even likely, true. An intelligence assessment will actually be telling you otherwise.

If the Resurrection of Jesus is not true, Christianity is not True

Before we assess the claim of the Resurrection of Jesus, let's visit just how crucial and central this belief is to Christianity. In 1st Corinthians 15:14-19, St. Paul states:

> **If Christ has not been raised, our preaching is useless and so is your faith. ... And if Christ has not been raised, your faith is worthless. ... If we have hope in Christ for this life only, we of all people are the most to be pitied.**

Nothing matches the sheer audacity of Christian claims, nor does any other religion depend so entirely on its truth claims as does Christianity. In short, to paraphrase St. Paul, if Jesus was not God and was not raised from the dead, then Christianity is a farce.

Believe *Because* We have Seen

As a person of faith, who has dedicated his life to the proposition that Jesus was, in fact, God and was raised from the dead, but who also has experience as an top secret intelligence officer, I am intrigued by the degree to which the very earliest sources for belief in the resurrection do not present it so much as an article of faith, but rather as something to be accepted based on reliable witness testimony.

It starts with the other apostles when they tell Thomas about it:

We have *seen* the Lord![116]

They do not tell Thomas Jesus has been raised from the dead and so he should believe that

---

[116] John 20:25.

doctrine as well. They tell him that they have *SEEN* him.

The fact of his actual death prior to resurrection is also presented in John as something to be accepted not as a point of faith, but because it is established by reliable witness testimony:

> When they came to Jesus and saw that he was already dead, they did not break his legs. But one soldier thrust his spear into his side and immediately there flowed out blood and water. **An eyewitness has testified, and his testimony is true. He knows that he speaks the truth, so that you also may believe.**[117]

The Gospel Message is continually grounded in the claim that it is reliable because of the sources that testify to it.

St. Paul describes in detail the people who serve as official witnesses of Jesus having been raised from the dead:

> He appeared to Kephas, then to the Twelve. After that he appeared to more than five hundred brothers at once, most of whom are still living,

---

[117] John 19:33-35.

though some have fallen asleep. After that he appeared to James, then to all the apostles.[118]

Dr. Keith Yandell, with whom I had the distinct privilege of studying in his class "Philosophy of Religion" at the University of Wisconsin-Madison, argued in his scholarship that, at a minimum, religious experience does constitute epistemological *evidence* for the object that was experienced. In other words, if someone has a vision of God, it does not prove God's existence. But it is still evidence that cannot be dismissed merely because the object of the experience is supernatural.[119]

And so, what do the claims of the witness to Jesus' resurrection mean? Dr. Yandell would assert that, at a minimum they certainly provide evidence, though not proof, that Jesus did rise from the dead.

---

[118] 1 Cor 15:5-7.

[119] Keith Yandell, *The Epistemology of Religious Experience* (Cambridge University Press, 1994).

The Reliability and Accuracy Assessment

In order to assess how reliable a human source of intelligence is, I remind you that NATO countries use what is termed the Admiralty Code. I will show you the letters and their definitions again so you can understand what the possible grades are. First, the source is assigned a letter based on their reliability. Here is a description of the letter grade:[120]

> **A - Completely reliable**: No doubt of authenticity, trustworthiness, or competency; has a history of complete reliability.
> **B - Usually reliable**: Minor doubt about authenticity, trustworthiness, or competency; has a history of valid information most of the time.
> **C - Fairly reliable**: Doubt of authenticity, trustworthiness, or competency but has provided valid information in the past.
> **D - Not usually reliable**: Significant doubt about authenticity, trustworthiness, or competency but has provided valid information in the past.
> **E - Unreliable**: Lacking in authenticity, trustworthiness, and competency; history of invalid

---

[120] US Army Field Manual 2-22.3, p. B1. https://fas.org/irp/doddir/army/fm2-22-3.pdf

information.
F - Reliability cannot be judged: No basis exists for evaluating the reliability of the source.

Notice here, the letters should not be considered "letter grades" as if it were a grade in school. This is strictly a ruling on how reliable a source is based on past performance. Arguably, a source termed "E" is to be trusted less than one with an "F," since the "E" source has previously demonstrated unreliability! And there is theoretically nothing preventing a human source, whose past performance has earned them an "A," from either intentionally or inadvertently passing on false information.

The F source is presumably brand new and we do not yet have any basis for assessing their reliability. Even though it has an "F," it might be entirely true. We just do not have any reason to trust it yet.

Next the actual information presented by the source is itself assessed for its accuracy, based on factors such as its confirmation by other sources, reasonableness, and consistency with other intelligence:[121]

---

[121] US Army Field Manual 2-22.3, p. 2.
https://fas.org/irp/doddir/army/fm2-22-3.pdf

1 - Confirmed by other sources: Confirmed by other independent sources; logical in itself; Consistent with other information on the subject.
2 - Probably True: Not confirmed; logical in itself; consistent with other information on the subject.
3 - Possibly True: Not confirmed; reasonably logical in itself; agrees with some other information on the subject.
4 - Doubtful: Not confirmed; possible but not logical; no other information on the subject.
5 - Improbable: Not confirmed; not logical in itself; contradicted by other information on the subject.
6 - Truth cannot be judged: No basis exists for evaluating the validity of the information.

Similarly with the reliability letters, note that number 6 here is simply a score assigned with no way to yet evaluate the information, whereas with 5 we presumably have other information which implies the data we are currently studying is probably not correct.

It must again be stated that a piece of information assigned what might be termed a "bad grade" could still be completely true. If a pathological liar tells you that it's raining, I wouldn't dismiss him despite the rain drops!

Should We Believe This?

In order to properly assess the overall veracity and reliability of the Apostles, we need to assess other claims they have made, apart from the Resurrection, and be able to either verify or refute them. But here's the problem. We do not have any other claims they have made.

One might here protest, saying that any and all historical details found in the Bible constitute apostolic claims. But this would be quite unfair. I mean, no one would imagine dismissing claims by the Roman historian Tacitus because we found an inaccuracy in the writings of the Roman historian Livy. In the same way, dismissing a claim found in the Gospel of Matthew because of an inaccuracy found in the book of Exodus would be ludicrous.

Perhaps one would then claim that an inaccuracy at least in the New Testament itself should constitute other testimony to assess the overall reliability of the Apostolic witness to the Resurrection. I would still here push back and point out that much less than half of the New Testament was written by people whom Church Tradition claims were original witnesses of the resurrected Jesus. St. Paul claims himself to be a witness to the Resurrected Jesus, but his claim is to have seen the Resurrected Jesus years later on the road to Damascus. Further, to hold any potential inconsistency found in the Gospel of Matthew against the claim of Matthew himself to have seen the risen Jesus means first accepting at face value the traditional attribution of that book to the Apostle Matthew.

No Basis Exists...

It would be tempting, as some scholars have done, to claim that the negative portrayal the New Testament makes, at times, about the Apostles themselves constitutes a secondary proof of their veracity. As the argument goes, who would paint themselves in such a bad light who was not otherwise telling you the whole truth? But to do so, I would have to be inconsistent on my earlier assertion that the overall text of the New Testament is not a source of further witness testimony.

And so, in the final analysis, lacking any substantial source of other claims the Apostles have made apart from the Resurrection of Jesus, I am forced to give them an Admiralty Grade of:

F - Reliability cannot be judged: No basis exists for evaluating the reliability of the source

But remember, a grade of "F" sounds bad only because it is the worst grade you can get in school. In the Admiralty Code, it is arguably a better grade than an "E."

Improbable and Illogical

Next we turn to the question of the *accuracy* of the Apostles' claim. The grade I must assign, while wearing the hat of a spy, is:

5 - Improbable: Not confirmed; not logical in itself; contradicted by other information on the subject

I would defend this grade as follows. The Resurrection of Jesus has certainly not ever been objectively confirmed by any source other than the New Testament. The Resurrection of Jesus is simultaneously both "not logical" and also "contradicted by other information on the subject "simply by the fact that no one has ever satisfactorily demonstrated that anyone resurrected from the dead.

Doubts and Impossibilities

As a spy, I've given the reliability and accuracy of the Apostles' claim to have seen the risen Lord a very low grade. But I want to remind you, the Admiralty Code ultimately does not assess whether a thing is true. It only assesses whether, based on the past performance of the source and the overall nature of the claim, it ought to be embraced as true.

We are left, just as St. Thomas was, with the question of whether to believe other people when they say that they saw the resurrected Jesus.

The Apostles tell us Jesus rose from the dead. But intelligence analysis would tell us that we should not accept their testimony as reliable or credible or accurate.

But Christian theologians recognized this fact early in Church history. The early Christian writer Tertullian[122] (155-240AD) famously wrote:

---

[122] You will perhaps notice that I did not give Tertullian the title "Saint." Despite his significant usefulness as a witness to early Christian thought, he left the mainstream (Catholic) Church to join a breakaway group called the Montanists.

And the Son of God died: it is credible because it is unfitting.
And having been buried he rose from the dead. **It is certain, since it is impossible**.
et mortuus est dei filius: credibile est, quia ineptum est.
et sepultus resurrexit: certum est, quia impossibile.[123]

After Jesus reportedly appeared to St. Thomas and that apostle finally believed, the Apostles tell us that Jesus said, "You believe because you have seen. Blessed are those who have not seen and yet believe."[124]

And so here we are. I could tell you that the fact that the Apostles died for their belief must count for something. But recent history tells us that people of many religions will die or even, sadly, kill for their faith.

Christ is Risen! Indeed He is Risen!

Did Jesus really rise from the dead?
I profess the doctrine that he did. I try to live

---

[123] Tertullian, *De Carne Christi* 5.

[124] John 20:29.

my life as if he did.

But on a human level, I do not know.

I cannot actually *know*.

I can only *believe*.

Or even just *hope*.

St. Paul wrote that "three things abide, faith, hope, and love. And the greatest of these is love" (1 Cor 13:13).

And so it would seem, from the way St. Paul ranked the three, that hope is greater even than faith.

But greater still than faith and hope—is love. I must love, and frequently it's very difficult, if I am to follow Jesus.

In the final analysis, believing the testimony of ancient Apostles that they saw the risen Jesus is not a compelling choice based on how the intelligence community would assess the reliability of the witnesses or their testimony. But yet, as these apostles travelled throughout their known world sharing this testimony, people believed them. And as the men and women who came to believe shared their belief, even after all the apostles had died out, mostly by martyrdom for their convictions, people continued to believe.

If a study of all this through intelligence analysis proves anything, it is that some intangible factor must account for belief in the Resurrection of Jesus being accepted and spreading the way it did.

The early Christian writer Tertullian, quoted earlier above, wrote how the Romans themselves noticed that "something else."

> See, they say, how they love each other.
> *vide, inquiunt, ut invicem se diligant.*[125]

It is love that animates that testimony. It is love that receives it. And that is because, it was Love that died on the Cross and rose again from the dead.

I do not believe in the Resurrection because it is logical, sensible, or rational. I believe it because, somehow, through the collective love of the generations of Christians who have lived for it and died for it, it is as if—I have witnessed it.

And so, despite not having seen the risen Lord with my physical eyes, as St. Peter did, this Easter (or as we Orthodox call it, Pascha), I give voice, having seen with the eyes of my heart, to the two thousand year old proclamation:

Christ is Risen! Indeed He is Risen!

---

[125] Tertullian, *Apologeticus pro Christianis* 38.

Chapter Nine: Cracking the Code of the Number 666

In this and the following two chapters of the book, I will present some of my original research, in which I apply my expertise, employing both biblical and intelligence methodologies to suggest solutions to some ancient biblical mysteries.

The Book of Revelation contains some of the most enigmatic topics of the New Testament. Who are the First and Second Beasts described in Revelation 13? And the most intriguing question of all—what is the name encoded in the number 666?

Where and When was the Book of Revelation Written?

The Book of Revelation was very likely among the last of the texts composed which would eventually end up in the Christian Canon of Scripture. Modern biblical scholars such as myself believe the evidence points to it being written sometime in the early 100's AD.

In Revelation chapters 2 and 3, seven churches are discussed. They are all situated in Western Asia Minor, modern day Turkey. The concern the author has for these places tells us that the book was very likely composed somewhere in that general area.

Speaking in very apocalyptic terms, the author of Revelation tells us:

> Then I saw a beast come out of the sea with ten horns and seven heads.[126]
> Then I saw another beast come up out of the earth. It wielded all the authority of the first beast.[127]
> ...and it made the earth and its inhabitants worship the first beast ... and it made anyone who did not worship the image of the beast to be put to death.[128]
> Let the one who has understanding calculate the number of the beast, for it is the number of a person and his number is 666.[129]

---

[126] Revelation 13:1.

[127] Revelation 13:12.

[128] Revelation 13:14-15.

[129] Revelation 13:18.

I believe, with many biblical scholars, that elements such as the First and Second Beast, as well as the number 666, were not meant to be guides for the end times. They were describing the author's contemporary concerns.

Revelation, Revealed...

By the accidents of history, there has been, preserved to this day, an exchange of letters between the Roman Emperor Trajan and a man named Pliny, who was the Roman governor of the Province of Bithynia and Pontus in Asia Minor in the year 110—around the time and in the general location where the Book of Revelation was likely written.

Pliny and the Christians

Pliny wrote to the Emperor Trajan asking for the Emperor's advice on how to deal with Christians. Pliny states that when someone was brought before him accused of being a Christian:

> **I interrogated them as to whether they were Christians**; those confessing I interrogated a second and a third time, having threatened them

with execution; **those persisting I ordered executed.**[130]

Pliny goes on to inform the Emperor that someone published an anonymous document naming a large number of people in his area as being Christians. Pliny interrogated the people named on the list and told the Emperor that he released any who:

> ...invoked the gods, following my words, and **made an offering of incense and wine to your image**, **which I had ordered to be brought for this purpose**, together with statues of the gods, and moreover cursed Christ.

Pliny/Trajan and the Book of Revelation

As I said earlier, the Book of Revelation states that the second beast:

> Makes as many as do not worship the image of the beast to be killed.[131]

---

[130] Pliny the Younger, *Epistulae* 10:96.

[131] Rev 13:15.

That is *exactly* what Pliny, writing at the same time and place as the author of Revelation, told his emperor that he was doing.

Revelation states, regarding the second beast:

> He exercises all the authority of the first beast in his presence.[132]

This certainly matches the authority that a Roman governor exercises in the name of the Emperor.

The seven heads likely signify the seven hills of Rome. If the seven heads are the seven hills of Rome, then perhaps the ten horns mean ten emperors.

In the year AD 69, following the death of Nero, three claimants to the imperial throne briefly reigned. They are not considered true Roman emperors. As of the year AD 110, when Pliny was governor in Asia Minor, Rome had seen the following true emperors:

---

[132] Revelation 13:12.

1) Augustus
2) Tiberius
3) Caligula
4) Claudius
5) Nero
6) Vespasian
7) Titus
8) Domitian
9) Nerva
10) Trajan

Nicomedia, the capitol of Bithynia and Pontus, where Pliny would have had his residence and base of operations, was just 250 miles from the center of the area where the Seven Churches of Asia mentioned in Revelation 2 and 3 are located. People in those Churches could not have been unaware of the persecution Pliny was overseeing just to their northeast. And they would have assumed that the Roman governor was carrying out the will of his superior far away in Rome.

The Number of the Beast

I assert that what Revelation 13 is describing is the persecution that Governor Pliny was conducting against Christians in his province in Asia Minor. And that would mean that Pliny is the second beast and so Trajan is the first. And the name Trajan, therefore, must be what is encoded by the number 666.

Some biblical scholars have previously asserted that the best candidate for the number 666 is the Emperor Nero, who ordered the first general persecution of Christians following the great fire of Rome in AD 64. The number 666 is found to match the Hebrew numerical values of the name Neron Caesar, the Greek version of his name, when written in Hebrew characters.

Here is a breakdown of the numbers for the characters of the name:

נרון קסר = Neron Kaisar = Nero Caesar
Nun (נ) = 50
Resh (ר) = 200
Waw (ו) = 6
Nun (נ) = 50
Qoph (ק) = 100
Samekh (ס) = 60
Resh (ר) = 200
And this adds up to 666.

There is a very old textual variant found among some manuscripts of Revelation, in which the number is 616 instead of 666.

And this variant may have come about because

that is the number produced when you calculate using Nero's Latin name, as follows:

נרו קסר = Nero Kaisar = Nero Caesar
Nun (נ) = 50
Resh (ר) = 200
Waw (ו) = 6
Qoph (ק) = 100
Samekh (ס) = 60
Resh (ר) = 200
Total = 616.

Now you will notice that the name Neron Caesar arrives at 666 as a fairly random collection of numbers. What if the author expected the reader to simply unpack the alphabetic values of the numbers 600, then something adding up to 60, and finally 6?

What is the Hebrew way to represent 600? The answer is:

Taw Resh (ת"ר) = TR

Taw (ת) equals 400 and *Resh* (ר) equals 200. They were used together by convention to signify 600.

The name *Traianus* in Latin or *Traianos* in Greek would be spelled next with the Hebrew *Yod*

(׳), producing the same Y sound as the Latin I before a vowel. And *Yod* equals 10.

The next consonant would be the *Nun* (נ). And *Nun* equals 50.

And so, TRYN (Traian) add up to 660. On to the final number. The Hebrew letter for 6 by itself was *Waw* (ו), the W sound, also used for the vowels O and U.

Taken all together, the number 666 encodes the Hebrew letters:

TRYNW   T R I N U   TRAIANU

Adding in the vowels, these letters are immediately recognizable as the name Traianus, Trajan. The sheer elegance of the number 666 would certainly be more important to the author of Revelation than the mere nominative form of his name, because adding the final S would have resulted in the inelegant number 726.

While that may be true, the context of Revelation 13:18 indicates that the form we have here may be precisely what we should have expected. The letters TRYNW would pronounce the Greek genitive form *Traianou*, "of Trajan."

The Greek word rendered as "number" (*ho arithmos*) can just as validly be translated as "sum." And in that case, the genitive form of the name Trajan would be expected, in parallel to the word *anthropou* "of a person":

arithmos gar anthropou esti
For it is the sum **of a person**.
kai ho arithmos autou χξς (666)
And its sum is—**of Trajan** (*Traianou*).

But I must address one final question. If this interpretation should have been apparent to early Christian readers, why was this solution not passed down as an option?

The answer comes in Trajan's response to Pliny's letter.

He wrote back the following:

[Christians] are not to be sought out; if they are denounced and found guilty, they must be punished... But anonymously posted accusations should have no place in any prosecution. For this is both a very bad example and not (in keeping with) our times.[133]

The early Christian Historian Eusebius states that, because of Trajan's reply to Pliny:

---

[133] Pliny the Younger, *Epistulae* 10:97.

On account of this, the persecution seemed lessened in its extreme violence.[134]

Trajan's reign was notable not only for its military expansion, but for internal prosperity enjoyed by all within the Empire. And as the memory of Pliny's persecution faded, esteem for Trajan only increased by the time of his death. Trajan was simply not an obvious candidate any more to be considered the Beast of the Apocalypse.

But I believe I have demonstrated that he was very likely the original man that the author of the Book of Revelation described as the first beast, and the man whose name was 666.

---

[134] Eusebius, *Church History* 3.33.2.

CHAPTER TEN:
KING DAVID: THE ORIGINAL GUITAR HERO

In this chapter I will propose a solution to a long standing linguistic mystery. There's a word in the Hebrew Bible, *selah* (סלה), for which commentators have proposed multiple interpretations. That's usually a sign that no one really knows what it means. I will argue that it is a borrowed word which means exactly the same thing as a word we borrowed into English centuries later.

A Musical Context

The word *selah* occurs three times in the book of Habakkuk and seventy-one times in the book of Psalms. Each time it shows up, it seems to mark some kind of break in the flow of what is being said. It seems to be somehow related to the musical nature of the Psalms as they were originally performed, such as a musical interlude. (Prophets like Habakkuk also performed their prophesies musically, as you can see from the description of Ezekiel as a singer in Ezekiel 33:32.)

The hero David was known to play a mean harp in his day.[135] When he has to flee from King Saul, one of the places he sojourns is the land of Philistia.[136]

We know very little about the Philistines and their language, though there is increasing consensus that the Philistines could have been an Indo-European speaking people who settled on the coast of the Mediterranean as part of the "Sea Peoples" phenomenon of the 2nd Millennium BC.

A Philistine Borrowing

Whenever peoples live beside each other, they may fight but they also exchange products and, eventually, words. I am proposing that the word *selah* is a borrowing from the Philistines. Now, I am not saying that King David himself is the one that brought it back or even that he necessarily

---

[135] See 1 Samuel 16:23.
[136] 1 Samuel 21.

wrote all of the Psalms attributed to him. (Though it does occur in many Psalms attributed to him.)[137]

So here's my theory. If Philistine is Indo-European and the word *selah* is a borrowing from them, it could be an etymological cognate to the word "*solo*." (The Proto-Indo-European root **solw-* carries the meanings of "whole" and "alone.")[138]

Musical notation is precisely where we tend to see word borrowing and then a tenacious preservation of terms. Notice how we still use Italian terms such as *fortissimo* and *crescendo*.

The possibility that *selah* indicated a musical interlude is not a new assertion. What I am saying, however, is that the word actually is related to the Italian word which we use even today to describe a musical *solo*.

Another Example

Another example of how musical words tend to be borrowed, not created, is found in the word for "harp" or "lyre." What David played on is called, in Hebrew, a *kinnor*. But the Greeks called their instrument a *kithara*. (The word may be also

---

[137] E.g., Psalms 3, 4, 9, 20, 21 et al.
[138] Cf., Latin *solus* 'alone' and Irish *slán* 'safe'.

related to the Old Persian *sithar*.) The Romans would borrow the word as *cithara*. It was borrowed by Semitic speaking peoples and shows up in Daniel 3:5 and the Odes of Solomon 6:1. It made its way into Arabic and then came back to Europe as ... "guitar!"

CHAPTER ELEVEN: THE SO-CALLED "HORNS" OF MOSES

In this chapter I will present a solution to another curious linguistic mystery. Exodus 34:29, 30, and 35 state that "the skin of Moses' face *qaran*." And *qaran* here is a verb meaning ... well, we do not know. Because it only occurs in this single passage, we have no further context. We do have a very common noun from this root, **qeren**, meaning 'horn'.

The rest of the passage describes that Moses, as result of whatever it was that *qaran* meant, would wear a veil (*masveh*) over his face. He would take off the veil when he spoke to God, but put it back on when in front of the Children of Israel. He did this because "the skin of Moses' face ... *qaran*." (Whatever *qaran* means.)

Already in ancient times, these verses were

generating confusion. The Greek LXX translation offers an interpretation when it renders the verb as *dedoxastai*, "was glorified."

St. Jerome translates the root based on the Hebrew noun and gives us the "horned face" (*faciem ... cornutam*) which is the basis of Michelangelo's famous statue.

Another ancient interpretation, generally followed in modern translations, is to view this as a verb meaning "to shine." This seems to have support in the use of the root in Habakkuk 3:4, where we read:

> His radiance is like light, he has two rays (*qarnayim*) coming from his hand.

The word rendered as "rays" (*qarnayim*) literally means 'two horns'. Perhaps this means bolts of lightning, which could resemble horns. So if this verb means something like "to send out rays" then we can translate the passage as "the skin of Moses' face shone."

This brings me to my new theory. While examining this matter, I spent some time considering a possible interpretation based on the same root in Arabic. This root primarily means "to connect, join." This gives us common words such as *muqaarana*, 'comparison', and *qarina*, 'wife' (i.e., joined one). The root also provides the same common noun as Hebrew; the Arabic word *qarn* means 'horn'.

But I was intrigued to discover that one possible form of this verbal root in Arabic (*istaqrana*)[139] has the meaning 'to produce pus', 'to come to a head (of boils)'.

We must always use caution when comparing the Hebrew and Arabic languages. But these languages are at least as related as, say, French and Italian. So a meaning in Arabic can be a valid window into the meaning of the same root in Hebrew.

This raises the startling possibility that the Hebrew *qaran* meant something like "to break out in boils" or "to run with pus." Indeed, it must be noted that the Hebrew text specifically describes this as something happening to Moses' *skin* (*'or*).

Regardless of the proposed theories on the meaning of the word, whatever condition Moses acquired seems to have been connected to his spending time in the very presence of God. It is not implausible that somehow being exposed to the divine presence affected the skin of his face in

---

[139] This is known as Form X.

some way.

This could also explain more directly why Moses is covering his face with some type of cloth when not in the presence of God. In addition to this condition possibly being a disfigurement, it required a cloth to treat the symptoms.

Exodus 34:30 states that the people "were afraid to draw near to [Moses]" because the skin of his face *qaran*. It is more likely that they were afraid to draw near to him because of a concern of catching what he had or because of revulsion at the sight of his condition. If his face was shining, they would have been afraid, to be sure. But the text specifically states that they were afraid "to draw near to him." This indicates fear of being near him, which was more likely as a result of a condition than merely his appearance.

It may be that this root meaning is what generates the meaning of 'horn'. A pastoral people certainly knew that animals are not born with horns. The horns sprout out of buds on the head much as a boil will mature and then produce a white surface before breaking.

At any rate, I am not aware of anyone previously proposing this solution on the basis of the Arabic root. This interpretation has the virtue of explaining the overall passage at least as well as a meaning "to shine." It also has cognate language support. But the clincher is that this solution alone accounts for the reality that *qaran* was affecting Moses' *skin* specifically. Elsewhere in the Bible, it is just faces themselves that shine, not the skin on them![140]

By the way, if you are ever in Rome, you can find Michelangelo's beautiful statue at an equally beautiful Church, St. Peter in Chains, just north of the Coliseum. Per Canon Law, there is no admission fee.

---

[140] Cf. Numbers 6:25; Matt 17:2.

Conclusion

In this book I have attempted to show how the tools of intelligence analysis can provide a fresh paradigm for better understanding the Bible. As an ancient document which is linguistically, topically, and chronologically diverse and complicated, I believe that intelligence analysis provides a valuable reality check on our limits in claiming to perfectly understand every word or even every page of Scripture.

I have stressed that the gold standard in confirming the veracity of information in the area of espionage is that happy moment when a fact can be independently confirmed by both HUMINT and SIGINT. Bringing this concept into the realm of the Bible, I have suggested that crucial pieces of Intel to better understand the biblical text have been preserved outside the Bible itself.

Just as a spy would gratefully use a SIGINT report to confirm what was reported by a human asset, so a reader of the Bible should happily explore information found in cognate languages, as well as the living traditions of the community that passed on the Bible, to arrive at a better understanding of what the biblical text is really saying.

I have explored matters that currently divide Protestants from Catholics and Orthodox, suggesting that a biblical defense of the latter can be discovered if we read the Bible in light of information passed down within the very community that meticulously and lovingly handed down the Scriptures to us.

The final word I will leave with you, however, is that, while there is value in learning *about* the Bible, nothing replaces just actually reading it! Read it through the tools I have discussed in this book. Do read it knowing the limitations any one translation may contain. Perhaps find in that fact the motivation to make an earnest attempt to learn one or more of the original languages! Seek out a variety of disciplines to better arrive at the truth of the text. But read the Bible. And may God bless your study of the Holy Scriptures.

www.ingramcontent.com/pod-product-compliance
Lightning Source LLC
Chambersburg PA
CBHW031441040426
42444CB00007B/926